MARK E. PETERSEN

A · B · I · O · G · R · A · P · H · Y

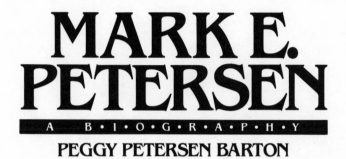

MARK E. PETERSEN

A · B·I·O·G·R·A·P·H·Y

PEGGY PETERSEN BARTON

Deseret Book

Salt Lake City, Utah

No part of this book may be reproduced in any
form or by any means without permission in writing
from the publisher, Deseret Book Company,
P.O. Box 30178, Salt Lake City, Utah 84130

First printing March 1985

Library of Congress Cataloging in Publication Data

Barton, Peggy Petersen, 1931–
    Mark E. Petersen.

    Includes index.
    1. Petersen, Mark E. 2. Mormon Church—Apostles—
Biography. 3. Church of Jesus Christ of Latter-day Saints
—Apostles—Biography. I. Title.
BX8695.P48B37 1985   289.3′32′0924 [B]   85-1659
ISBN 0-87747-642-X

Contents

Mark E. Petersen

by Elder Thomas S. Monson
of the Council of the Twelve

"Here and there, and now and then, God makes a giant among men." Such a giant among men was Elder Mark E. Petersen. He personified righteousness, he exemplified industry, he demonstrated love. How he will be missed in mortality!

Few men are given the opportunity to influence the Church in the manner in which Elder Mark E. Petersen influenced it for nearly forty years as one of the Lord's special witnesses.

His was a pen of spiritual power. Mark Petersen combined an insightful mind with a faith-filled heart to work wonders with his words. His style was distinctively his own. The many years he worked as a reporter and editor showed in the crispness of his sentences, the probing and succinct questions that punctuated his messages, and the conclusions of his appeals, which invariably penetrated the heart of the reader and prompted a determination to come closer to Christ.

With rare exceptions, he wrote every editorial for the *Church News* during its fifty-three years. During World War II, for over four years he personally did almost all the writing and editing for a twelve-page monthly servicemen's *Church News.*

Note: These comments have been excerpted from "Mark E. Petersen: A Giant Among Men," *Ensign*, March 1985, pp. 6-13. Used with permission.

During his service in the Council of the Twelve, Elder Petersen authored more than forty books, primarily on gospel themes—one for each year he served. In addition, he, with his beloved wife Emma Marr Petersen, co-authored a number of titles that found popular appeal and wide distribution. To this array could be added dozens of pamphlets, scores of articles, and hundreds of messages, all written to foster faith.

To match the persuasion of his written words, Mark E. Petersen was endowed with a rich and resonant baritone voice with which he proclaimed the word of God at home and abroad all the days of his life. He was a man of courage, a man of faith, a man of ability, a man of service, a man of love, a man of God. Indeed, Mark E. Petersen was "a man for all seasons."

I like the way another member of the Twelve, Elder Richard L. Evans, once described him: "Mark E. Petersen, of the Council of the Twelve, is a sincerely modest man, humble of heart, but of great courage and competence and a capacity for work which drives him, as he in turn drives himself—ceaselessly it seems."

With the call to the apostleship came added responsibility and the assignment to let his voice be heard and his influence felt throughout the entire earth. In the forty years he served in the Twelve, Mark visited a good share of the stakes and most of the missions of the world. Wherever he went, his indelible impression has remained.

Above all, his calling as an apostle of the Lord sealed his powerful trust in God with a certainty that was inspiring. Once, a government leader in a country distant from the United States heard Elder Petersen speak and said, "That man has inner authority—the kind of which I have never seen before. If I were a Christian, I would say God saved him for a special time and a special work."

Those who heard Elder Mark E. Petersen's voice and those who read his words could readily see that here was a fearless defender and testifier of truth, intelligent in thought, radiant and warm in personality, succinct and powerful in expression, unwavering and unflinching in commitment and belief. He could teach, persuade, warn, explain, and encourage. He was a most able exponent of Church doctrines and programs. His was an ability to make complex things simple and easily understood, often through the use of questions to identify a specific point for discussion.

Yet, with all of his faith, commitment, and energy, he was, as President Ezra Taft Benson has said, "one of the most kind, considerate, and gracious men I have known." Graciousness was truly a dominant characteristic of Mark Petersen. From it flowed his refinement, his appreciation for education, for art, and particularly for music.

Easy it is to see why so many who knew him well loved him so dearly. He was, as a fellow member of the Twelve said, "a fair judge, a tireless worker," and "a compassionate comforter of the sorrowing, a champion of those who have earnestly repented of mistakes, a persistent pursuer of the facts." A lifelong friend said, "I have never known Mark to do a cheap or shoddy or mean thing." He was a man of full integrity, firm loyalty, personal courage, and great faith.

I loved, respected, and admired Mark Petersen for these and many other traits and for his life of devotion to truth and to duty. These are seen as old virtues by many in our time, but they are virtues ever so dear to our Father in heaven. As age crept up on him (could one really think of Mark's energetic nature controlled by age?), sickness and attendant complications did what age alone could not. Even so, with gallant vigor he carried on until the end.

He is now with his dear Emma Marr, his companion with whom he created one of the greatest loving husband and wife relationships I have ever seen. They were equally yoked in faith and commitment and in their love of family, of music, and of the songs of Zion, which they sang together again and again.

We have been a blessed people to have had him for nearly forty years as one of our prophets, seers, and revelators. He was a "giant" here. We miss him. He is a "giant" there. They welcome him. Our beloved Mark has gone home.

Acknowledgments

Following the death of my father, as hundreds of messages revealed the ways in which he had touched the lives of others, I realized that his desire for privacy had concealed the real Mark E. Petersen from many of those around him. His passions for astronomy and scripture research, his enjoyment of poetry and music, his devotion to "today's news today," his remarkably quick wit, his instinctive courtesy and kindness remained hidden from all but a few. His motto "No Time to Lose" in its gold frame on a bookshelf seemed to urge me to my typewriter. On his desk lay a passage from Wordsworth's "Prelude," marked in his familiar hand:

> *Then was the truth received into my heart*
> *That under heaviest sorrow earth can bring,*
> *If from the affliction somewhere did not grow,*
> *Honor which could not else have been,*
> *A faith, an elevation, and a sanctity.*

Sincere thanks to all who shared personal glimpses; to Dorene and Charles Beagles for endless hours of toil albeit a labor of love; to Stanley D. Neeleman for professional assistance; to Elder Thomas S. Monson and Wendell J. Ashton for encouragement and kindness; to my children—Mark for his work on the missionary journals, Sydney and Bob, Tony and Drew for ideas and impressions; to Uncle Claude, Aunt Mona, and Aunt Phoebe for priceless childhood recollections; and especially to Eleanor Knowles for her skillful editing of this volume and many other writings of the subject of this biography.

1

The Twins

Presidential election day, November 6, 1900, held no fascination for Christine Marie Andersen Petersen as she sat next to the coal stove in her kitchen. With almost invisible stitches she fashioned a gown for the baby whose imminent appearance had swollen her tiny figure to amazing proportions. Contentedly she watched her two small sons as they played with blocks of wood left over from their father's building business.

A knock at the front door interrupted her reveries. It was Brother Rushton, the driver of the voting surrey. In 1900, without transportation to the polls, few voters cast their ballots. Salt Lake City provided a way to and from the voting places, thus allowing the citizenry to participate in elections. A surrey pulled by two smart horses waited in front of the house.

Christine, in her very uncomfortable condition, had no desire to climb up into the surrey. With her two previous pregnancies she had moved about freely, carrying on her life without such discomfort, but now she spent her days next to the fire rocking and sewing. However, Chris and Claude, her two little boys, begged for a ride with Brother Rushton. Going to vote was almost easier than explaining to her sons that their mother was too great with child to move from her chair.

As he helped Christine and her children into the surrey, Brother Rushton felt sorry for the little Danish woman. With her shawl she made a noble attempt to hide her enormous

1

body. He hoped she wouldn't have her baby before he could return her to her home. Luck was with them, and Christine voted in a presidential election that would make history, for William McKinley defeated William J. Bryant by the largest popular vote ever recorded in the United States.

But the trip in the surrey had taken its toll. By evening Christine knew the baby was on its way, and early the next morning, November 7, 1900, Mrs. Lindberg, the midwife, arrived at the Petersen home. Christine endured her third labor stoically. With two young sons, a devoted husband, and a new two-room house, life was good. Her childhood in Denmark seemed so long ago . . .

Born to Bertrum Andersen and Marie Elisabeth Nielsen on November 1, 1872, at Hvorup, Denmark, Christine had loved her home on her father's prosperous farm and especially Sundays in the Lutheran Church. When she was seven, a country school became the dominant influence in her life. The all-male staff ruled their charges with the proverbial iron hand, demanding long hours of study from 9 A.M. to 4 P.M. every day but Sunday. Eagerly the students looked forward to August, when a month's vacation relieved them of their books. At Christmastime, while dining tables groaned beneath traditional Danish delicacies, two weeks of daily church attendance rescued the children from the stern schoolmasters. Everyone attended church every day during this yuletide holiday, culminating in special midnight worship services on Christmas Eve. It was a time for eating and churchgoing, but contrary to custom in the United States, no gifts were given. Christine never owned a doll. A jumping rope and a rubber ball were her only toys in spite of the wealth of her family.

At sixteen she finished school and was confirmed a member of the Lutheran Church by her minister. For this occasion, the girls wore ankle-length black dresses and the boys sported their first long trousers.

After graduation she traveled to Aalborg and stayed with

a married sister while completing two years of dressmaking training. Her older brother, Ferdinand, also moved to Aalborg, where he met a beautiful young Mormon girl named Agnes Andersen. They soon fell in love. Agnes converted Ferdinand, and he was baptized a member of The Church of Jesus Christ of Latter-day Saints. He served a one-year home mission in Aalborg, preaching the gospel to all who would listen, including his sister. Christine joined the Church, and together they went to the Mormon meetings, associating with a fine group of young people.

Ferdinand borrowed money from his father for his passage to the United States and traveled to America with two missionaries. A talented inventor, he made a comfortable income and soon could repay his debts and send money to his sweetheart, Agnes, for her passage to Zion. He hoped to marry her. But when she arrived, Agnes had changed her mind about the romance, so Ferdinand wrote to his parents and asked that Christine be allowed to join him in Salt Lake City. After several letters describing the wonders of the new land, Ferdinand persuaded his father to allow Christine to leave Denmark. Christine and Ferdinand were the only members of their family who joined the Church. With the money provided by her parents, she was able to travel second-class with the missionaries instead of the steerage endured by so many Saints.

When Christine arrived in Utah, she joined her brother in a rooming house run by a Mrs. Andersen in Salt Lake City. She wasn't happy and didn't like life in this strange land, but she had no money to return to Denmark. To her, the desert seemed barren and dry after the lush foliage of her birthplace.

But full of Danish determination, she made the best of her situation and began to earn her living by dressmaking. During the winter she worked for the Mehesy Furrier Shop on the northeast corner of State Street and Broadway, where the Centre Theater would later be erected. When the tem-

Christine Andersen,
Mark's mother, at age
seventeen, shortly
after she arrived in
Salt Lake City

perature rose and the fur business faltered, Christine sewed
frocks for the females of prominent families in the city.

During this period the Danish-speaking members met
for church services in the Assembly Hall on Temple Square.
Memories of the old country drew these converts together as
they partook of the sacrament and studied their new religion. One day Christine noticed a handsome, tall, dark-
haired young man with sparkling green eyes and a strong
singing voice. For several Sundays she watched with interest
as the fervent immigrant so obviously enjoyed the services.
Christine asked a friend to introduce them. The young man
had joined the Church as a child in Denmark, and his whole
family had come to Zion. His name was Christian Petersen,
and he was the brother of her landlady.

In 1877, when Christian's father, Hans, was a young man
with a small family in Soro, Denmark, a Mormon elder came
to his home one day asking for shelter. The missionary was

admitted, and after some conversation he suggested that a cottage meeting be held there. Hans granted permission and then traveled all about the countryside on horseback, inviting his neighbors to attend the meeting. A large crowd collected, but not all were friendly. While many came into the house and listened attentively to the elder, a greater number remained outside creating a noisy disturbance. Finally the dissenters pounded on the door and demanded that the elder be turned over to them for tarring and feathering. Christian's father declared that the elder would remain in safety under his roof until the mob dispersed, even if it meant staying the night. Then Hans nailed the front door shut and, standing at the back door of his house with a large gun, urged the elder to continue his message. The ringleaders tried to force their way into the little home, but the look in Hans's eye and the rifle in his hands persuaded them that they should remain outside.

At the conclusion of the elder's talk, those attending the meeting returned to their homes. The mob continued to wait, as did Hans and the gun. At about two in the morning, still standing guard, Hans watched as the mob melted away into the night. Then, under cover of darkness, he took the elder behind him on his horse and rode to the young man's lodgings.

The people who had made up the mob were enraged at Hans, but he and his wife continued to investigate the gospel despite the abuse heaped upon them and their little family. A year later, after much study and prayer, the parents decided to become members of The Church of Jesus Christ of Latter-day Saints. But how could they be baptized? Because of the bitterness of their neighbors, the Petersens were threatened with physical violence if they appeared in any public place with the elders. Still, they desired baptism.

One night at midnight the young couple and the elder went to a large hole in the ground made by farmers carrying away the rich soil. Seepage had filled the hole with water. In this water Hans and his wife were baptized. Then they hurried home, where they were confirmed in the early morning hours. Despite cruelty and threats, these valiant souls began to preach the gospel, spreading the word to all who would listen. Through their labors a branch of the Church was formed with Hans as president. He headed the Soro Branch until his immigration to Utah.

Christian Petersen was born July 13, 1870, in Lindebjerg, Soro, Denmark, the son of Hans and Kirstine Jeppesen Petersen. His mother became a strong preacher of Mormonism. Though his father did much preaching, his mother was the real expert on the scriptures.

The only school available to Christian was a Lutheran Church school. If he belonged to any other than the state religion, he could not finish his education. Christian was eight years old when his parents became Mormons, and from that time he spoke of his testimony of the truth of the gospel with great fervor for a child. But his baptism was postponed until he had completed his schooling. He became a Mormon when he was fifteen. His three sisters also joined the Church.

The little family gave freely of their time and finances in support of their new religion. They provided a place to stay for the elders who traveled without purse or scrip. The Petersens journeyed many miles to attend church meetings until Hans became branch president; then the services were held in their home. During Christian's boyhood, he worked with his father manufacturing charcoal. In the last two years that the family lived in Denmark, with his schooling completed, Christian made the charcoal and his father went from town to town selling it.

The Hans Petersen family had a great desire to come to Zion. Finally enough money had been put aside. Christian, the youngest child, would accompany his parents to the United States. The three sisters preceded them, joining other groups of Saints. With his parents, Christian started the long journey when he was seventeen. The plan called for a stop of one week in Liverpool to rest before the arduous sea voyage.

*Hans and Kirstine
Petersen with their son
Christian (Mark's father),
photographed in Soro,
Denmark, before they
emigrated to Utah*

Arriving there, the three travelers began walking toward their hotel. However, Kirstine was jostled by the crowds and became separated from her husband and son. When she realized that she was lost, she approached a policeman in much fear and confusion and poured out her troubles to him. He took her to the hotel, where Hans and Christian waited anxiously. She felt it a great blessing that in such a large city she would be led to the one policeman who could understand her language, for the policeman was also a native of Denmark.

Seven delightful days in Liverpool were followed by eleven rough days on the ship *Nevada*. But seasickness and discomfort were forgotten as the family boarded the train for Tempe, Arizona. From Tempe they traveled to Mesa, where they waited for the sisters to join them. Finally reunited, the Petersens moved to Salt Lake City in 1890.

As a result of their association at the Assembly Hall, the friendship between Christine Marie Andersen and Christian

*Christine and
Christian Petersen
with their firstborn
son, Chris, 1895*

Petersen blossomed into a very loving relationship. On January 23, 1893, they were married. Christian was ordained an elder July 8, 1895, and the couple were sealed in the Salt Lake Temple on December 11, 1895 . . .

Now, as her labor pains grew longer and harder, Christine felt grateful that her husband was able to provide her with a midwife. As Mrs. Lindberg wiped her brow and held her hand, Christine wondered if the baby were a boy or a girl. Christian, Jr., and Claude wanted a baby sister.

Mark Edward Petersen made his debut into the world with a lusty wail on Wednesday morning, November 7, 1900. Two uncomfortable hours later, Mona Elisabeth joined her twin. Chris and Claude had both a brother and a sister! Mrs. Lindberg stayed to help the surprised parents during the first week. For the delivery and seven days of postnatal care, she received ten dollars, five dollars for each baby.

During the first few months of their lives, the Petersen twins were placed in a rocking cradle built by their father for the occasion. Fortunately he had made the cradle as large as a crib, and Mark Edward and Mona Elisabeth lay with their feet together and their heads on either end. November was cold, and the only heat in the house at 744 West Seventh South came from a small coal stove. There were no electric lights; kerosene lamps provided illumination. The two-room brick structure had a lumber shanty at the side. Christian, a carpenter, had built the little home with love for and in anticipation of the new arrival—and now the family was doubly blessed with two babies!

With only a few homes on the entire block, the neighborhood was not densely populated. Across the street to the south was a ten-acre plot with no houses on it. Many years later this area became Welfare Square in Salt Lake City. The Petersen family home, now painted white, still stands just north of the square.

In his personal history, Mark later wrote about his early life: "The ushering into mortality of myself and my sister was amid most humble circumstances. My mother tells me that I was a big and bad baby. My twin sister, although quite as large as myself, was a very good baby and gave her little trouble. My mother often said she wouldn't wish her worst enemy to have twins.

"My earliest recollections are of playing with my twin sister. She was my first playmate and closest playmate. She was my constant companion right up to the time of her marriage. Twins we were in spirit as well as in flesh, for we grew up together, went through school together, in the same rooms together, went to parties and the theater together, and much preferred dancing together than with others. In fact, we were inseparable."

At the time of Mark and Mona's birth, their father was employed by the Utah Light and Railway Company, which later became the Utah Light and Traction Company. The company operated a streetcar system in Salt Lake City.

Later he sought employment with the Denver and Rio Grande Railroad, building freight cars. He was a talented car-

penter and could make anything with his hands. Not satisfied
to work for others, he bought a set of books called *The Steel
Square,* which he studied diligently, learning how to build
houses with skill.

With four children and a husband to care for, Christine
had little time for her own pleasure. The twins were certainly
healthy, but as soon as she rocked Mona to sleep, Mark, complaining loudly, would waken her. Without a washing
machine, twins seemed a trial. However, soon the babies
amused each other, and life was easier to endure.

In the ten-acre field across the street, the children could
play happily without disturbing the neighbors. Then why did
Mark always seem to be in trouble? Such an active boy, so
curious, so strong—why couldn't he be more placid like
Mona? When the boys in the neighborhood leaned a board
against the Petersen fence to use as a slide, it was Mona who
returned the tearful Mark to the comfort of Mama's arms and
held her twin's hand as, upended on his mother's lap, he had
the slivers removed from his bared bottom.

A small hill was used for sleigh riding in the winter, and
a little lake froze for ice skating. Fires at the edge of the lake
dried damp fingers and toes. In the summer the sparkling
clean waters of the Jordan River offered swimming and
fishing.

Almost from the time of their birth, Christine counted
the days until the twins could attend school. There were no
kindergartens, and pupils must be six to be admitted. But
their mother was desperate. Mona and Mark would be six on
November 7, and they were quite large for their age. Christine dressed them for learning and delivered them to the
door of Riverside School on Eighth West, where eight grades
were taught.

As Mark and Mona walked slowly down the hall, the basement door swung open and out stepped the school janitor,
an ugly little man covered with soot from a recent struggle
with the furnace. Certain that this character from Grimm's

fairytales intended to harm them, the twins screamed in horror and tearfully ran all the way home.

"We received no hearing to our plea to be allowed to remain at home and forget school," Mark wrote, "but we were promptly marched right back by our mother and placed in the care of the teacher. Our grade-school days as viewed in memory now are just a maze of snowball fights, marble games, volleyball, basketball, football, and the three r's, with the three r's most dim in the picture."

One memorable summer's day Claude decided to walk along the board at the top of the Petersen fence. He lost his balance and fell head down with his feet wedged between the pickets. He could neither reach the ground nor lift himself up, so he hung upside down hollering. The noise did little good until a streetcar came along. The motorman observed Claude hanging by his toes, stopped the car, lifted the tearful boy to the ground, returned to his streetcar, and continued on his way.

Christine Petersen and her four children: twins Mark and Mona, age 1; Chris (back), and Claude, 1901

Mischief continually dogged Mark's footsteps. A house was being moved, a slow, arduous procedure with a wagon. When the driver parked his rig near the Petersen house for the night, he had no way of knowing that in spite of Mona's pleas, Mark's passion for rock-throwing would overcome his good sense. Rocks had always attracted Mark. All through his life he liked to see how far he could throw one. He liked to aim at targets. He liked to skip rocks on water. And he liked having contests with his friends. He promptly invited all the young neighborhood boys his age to a rock-throwing spectacular. No one meant to break any windows; they only wanted to see how close they could come. But somehow the windows were shattered and five little boys found themselves in court, where a solemn judge ordered them to make restitution. For months, every cent that passed through Mark's hands, minus tithing, bought windows to pay for his great adventure.

The Petersen family kept chickens and pigeons. The chickens laid eggs anywhere but in their nests, and the children had daily egg hunts during the warm summer months. The pigeons were raised to provide food. They reproduced rapidly but the children balked at eating their pets.

Children's diseases could be a problem to a family with four active little ones. Mona recalls this incident: "We had a nurse when we caught scarlet fever and she was a terror. If Mark got near anything she would get after him. There was a teakettle boiling on the stove, and Mark kept putting his hands over it to get warm. She made him go away so the germs wouldn't get in the boiling water. I brought scarlet fever home from school to the rest of the children. Then Chris got appendicitis. He had a real bad time. The doctors put him on the dining room table and operated on him. He nearly died. He had peritonitis, and a tube drained the poison. Mark and Claude had scarlet fever real bad too."

Baptism was a special time in the lives of the Petersen children. The story of Hans and Kirstine Petersen, their conversion, and their baptism in a hole in the earth held special fascination for Mark and Mona, who never tired of listening to the tale. On Saturday, December 5, 1908, the twins were baptized in the font in the Salt Lake Tabernacle by Andrew Mollerup. They were confirmed by their father, Christian Petersen, in the old 26th Ward Chapel the next day.

2

The Growing Years

"If ye shall ask with a sincere heart"
(Moroni 10:4)

Mark's devotion to the scriptures and hunger to learn all they might offer added a new dimension to his life. He longed to go on a mission, preferably to Denmark to teach all his relatives who had not joined the Church. He knew that he could bring many souls to an understanding of the gospel. (He was to be disappointed on both counts, for he would be called to Canada, not Denmark, and as he often told his family, his feet never got wet in the waters of baptism.)

On April 8, 1909, the twins woke in confusion and alarm. Their mother had become very, very ill. A doctor was hurriedly summoned, and their father sent them to the home of their Aunt Emma Andersen at Eighth West and Second South. No explanation was given, and Mark and Mona became very frightened. A few hours later, their father came to take them back home.

Mark wrote of this experience, "I recall walking into the front room of that home and seeing my mother in a large white bed which they had at that time. We kids were invited to come alongside the bed and see the little daughter born to my mother that day. The new little girl was Phoebe, my sister. Of course, we were all very happy.

"My first clear recollection concerning Phoebe following her birth is that she became quite ill in her earliest infancy. She lay sick in a large old-fashioned baby buggy borrowed from my Aunt Minnie Hansen. I believe she was suffering from chickenpox or measles. I recall how one day I came running into the front room and surprised my mother, who

was standing beside the buggy in which little Phoebe lay. My
mother was weeping over Phoebe's condition. I remember
the embarrassment I felt on finding my mother weeping. It
was the first time as far as I can remember that I had ever
seen her weep."

With the new addition to the Christian Petersen family,
the house needed to be remodeled. It became a fine red-
brick structure with a modern porch and sleeping porch and
a summer kitchen in the rear. In the backyard, a wooden
floor, eight by ten feet, with wood walls three feet high, was
topped by a tent. The boys slept outside in this tent-house
during the summer.

In the winter, with no room in the main part of the
house, Chris, Claude, and Mark slept on the sleeping porch
with the screens covered with canvas to keep out snow and
ice. Unfortunately the canvas did not keep out the cold. The
children became proud owners of an English sheep dog
named Jingo. Claude and Mark, who slept together in the
same bed, trained Jingo to retire an hour before their bed-
time to warm the bed. On very cold nights they heated bricks
in the oven of their mother's coal stove and placed them between the freezing sheets.

Mona remembers that she had to sleep on a couch in the
front room. "When we had visitors we built a fire in the fire-
place, and I would lie in bed and watch the glowing coals. It
was really pretty. There was a dining room that had a couple
of cots in it as well, and a bedroom for our parents. The bathroom was a little house outside in the backyard. Mark and I
were eighteen before we had a bathroom inside the house.
There was a washstand in the kitchen where the family
washed in the mornings. We bathed in a galvanized washtub
in the kitchen. There was no privacy. We just kind of took it
for granted and didn't think about it. Even when I was older
I just stood at the washstand and washed."

The Petersen house stood fairly close to the railroad
tracks. Transients often jumped from slow-moving trains and
called at the little home, begging for food. A great lesson in

charity was taught to the children, for Christine never once failed to fill a nice plate with good hot food to feed these men. No matter how little the Petersens had, there was enough to share with someone less fortunate.

In the backyard of the Petersen home stood a little shop where Christian did much of the cabinet work for the homes he was now building. It was in this shop that the three Petersen brothers first learned to use carpenters' tools skillfully. During the summer vacations Chris, Claude, and Mark spent part of their time as carpenters' apprentices with a wage of one dollar a day.

As Christian's building business flourished, he hired an old Dane to work on his cabinets. This elderly gentleman was an expert cabinetmaker and did outstanding work, especially when one considered that he made his tools by hand, carefully crafting his own planes and chisels. The three boys spent hours watching as he lovingly fashioned beautiful cabinets. A young German immigrant painted the houses that Christian built. He was an excellent artist and did lovely work, but the paint fumes seemed to have affected his health and his mental condition. He had painters' colic. At times he seemed very strange, but he was always happy and agreeable.

Since he had no electric tools, Christian had to stand for many days sawing rafters and joists by hand. He brought his saws home at night to sharpen them, and the three boys watched and learned.

As the boys grew older and able to take on a little responsibility, their father took them to his work on the days they were not attending school, getting them out of their mother's way and using their energy to help in the building business.

At that time most homes in Salt Lake City had full basements, dug by hand with a pick and a shovel. Usually the shape followed the outline of the house with a depth of about four feet. Since no cement mixers were available, Christian made a wooden platform on which he and the three boys mixed by hand the proper amounts of sand, gravel, cement, and water, which they shoveled into wheelbarrows and pushed to fill the forms. It was hard, backbreaking work.

Church attendance offered many interesting diversions. One was in the form of the Sunday School organist, a scrawny eight-year-old boy. The Petersen children liked to watch him climb up on the organ stool to play the music. The little boy's name was Alexander Schreiner. Sacrament was a holy ordinance—and sometimes a dangerous one. The water was passed around in one glass for all, and colds, flu, and other communicable diseases "blessed" the ward members. Each person tried to take his sip on a place where no other lip had touched. Even the bravest souls wiped the glass before they partook.

Central heating in a meetinghouse was unheard of. One large potbelly stove served the congregation. Curtains were drawn in the amusement hall for classrooms, and if the Petersen children didn't like their own Sunday School lessons, they could just listen to the teacher on the other side of the curtain. Christian taught the parents' class in Sunday School and the deacons and teachers classes in priesthood meeting.

The Hans Petersens, the grandparents, lived between Seventh and Eighth West on Genessee Avenue, where they had a little farm with two cows, a pretty but mean horse, chickens, and ducks. Grandpa Hans, despite his commitment to the Church, seemed to overlook some of its precepts, particularly the Word of Wisdom. He used to like a little drink of schnapps if he woke during the night. He claimed it helped him relax and go back to sleep. He kept a bottle just beneath his bed so he could reach it without getting up. One day his wife had been cleaning the furniture with turpentine in an old schnapps bottle. After polishing the nightstand, she set the bottle down by the side of the bed, thinking she would put it away later. Somehow she forgot. During the night

Grandpa Hans woke, reached for his schnapps bottle, and took a long drink of turpentine. He was very sick as a result, but he no longer felt the need for schnapps.

The Petersen children enjoyed family gatherings with their cousins. At Christmas and Thanksgiving dinners, the adults ate at the first setting of the table. Then, when their meal had been cleared away, the children sat down to a big feed. Uncle Lars's place on Redwood Road was a special delight. He had two beautiful roan-colored horses that he used to pull his "oil wagon," from which he sold kerosene door to door. Sometimes he used his horses to pull his beautiful surrey with white fringe around the top. Occasionally he let the Petersen children have a ride in the surrey.

Uncle Lars had a ten-acre farm and a large home. In the wintertime the children walked from the end of the streetcar line through knee-deep snow to visit Uncle Lars, who played the accordian and raised chickens, pigs, and vegetables. In the fall when he killed a pig, he always gave Christine half the head to make headcheese, a great delicacy. Pig's liver also guaranteed a wonderful meal.

School demanded much time in the winter, but in summertime Christian rewarded the boys for their work as carpenters' apprentices by taking them to Calder's Park, now Nibley Park Golf Course, where a large wooden saucer with motorcycle races added to the excitement. The family also enjoyed the Salt Palace, a resort at Ninth South and Main Street, where Mark loved to look at the real palace of salt, watch bicycle races, and listen to Held's Brass Band. Whenever Mr. Held played a trumpet solo, the audience cheered. The Petersen children were very sad when a fire swept through this resort and it was abandoned.

It may have been listening to Held's Brass Band that planted the seed for Mark and Claude to seek musical training. Mark attempted to conquer the baritone horn, while Claude played a slide trombone. In his pursuit of excellence, Mark rode his bike, carrying his baritone horn under his arm, to Seventeenth South and Ninth East for a weekly music lesson financed by his two paper routes. Occasionally Claude and Mark were invited to play at a ward social or Mutual Improvement Association meeting, but only when no other "talent" could be found. The result was unforgettable and regrettable.

Every fourth of July the Petersens and all the aunts and uncles and cousins met at Liberty Park for a big family picnic. Often the world's heavyweight championship took place on that holiday. With neither radio nor television, the men waited anxiously for the paperboys to come to the park shouting, "Extra! Extra! Read all about it!" The men all bought papers, studied them, and then sat on the lawn discussing the details of the fight.

Christine and Christian belonged to a Danish lodge made up of members of the Church who had come from Denmark. The group held many social events and parties, some of which the children could attend. Every Christmas a huge celebration was planned for the entire family, with a big Christmas tree touching the ceiling and covered with tiny lighted candles. Santa Claus appeared, and music, dancing, and games filled the evening.

As her children needed her less, Christine began again to sew professionally. Mona remembers that her mother often sat up late to finish an order for a customer. Once while pressing an elaborate party dress, Christine accidentally scorched it and had to hurry to buy matching fabric and repair the frock. Christine did not teach her daughters to sew, not even to run a sewing machine. Mona thought it was because she did not want to see her daughters working as hard as she had done. Christine made all the family's clothing, including their winter coats. A neighbor knit their hats, stockings, and mittens.

When he was ten years old, Mark went to a sacrament meeting that changed his future. Elder Heber J. Grant of the Council of the Twelve was the speaker. Elder Grant would become President of the Church and as such would issue a call to Mark Edward Petersen to the Council of the Twelve. In his sacrament meeting talk he told of the wonders to be found in the Book of Mormon, and especially of Nephi and his courage. Mark could hardly wait to read of the boy born of goodly parents, like himself, and who dared to stand alone in obedience to God.

Mark had always been a good reader and had done well in school. Now he became a serious student of the scriptures, a habit that was to remain with him throughout his life. All the energy and curiosity that had led him into trouble in his earlier years was now focused on discovering who he was and where he had come from. He understood also where he wanted to go.

The Petersen family read the scriptures daily and attended church. Blessed with a pleasant singing voice, Mark enjoyed choruses and choirs as well as solos. When friends gathered, singing songs often filled a summer's evening or a cold winter night. His favorite was "A Mormon Boy." When he came to the words, "My father was a Mormon true and when I am a man, I want to be like him and do just all the good I can," a new meaning emerged. Mark loved his father, who was strong and good and had taught him so many things and given him life. But at this time he also became aware of his Father in heaven and of a strong relationship and responsibility to do His will. As he sang of his father, "I want to be like him and do just all the good I can," he saw his Heavenly Father as a pattern.

In 1913, when he was twelve years of age, Mark was appointed president of the 26th Ward deacons quorum and became a boy scout. The scout organization at this time was just in its infancy, and few got very far in it. He passed the tenderfoot examination, got his badge, and then immediately was made the assistant scoutmaster. But about that time a new scoutmaster was appointed who let the organization go to rack and ruin, and thus ended Mark's scouting days.

Mark's priesthood instructor almost throughout his Aaronic Priesthood period was his father. Christian ordained Mark a deacon on September 25, 1911; the boy turned twelve

Mark's eighth-grade graduation photo

on November 7 a year later. Christian was the instructor of the deacons quorum and the teachers quorum. He assisted also while Mark was a priest. He ordained Mark a teacher on February 8, 1915, still in the 26th Ward. For some reason that Mark could not remember, his father did not ordain him a priest. Frank A. Proctor, an Englishman with whom Mark sang in the choir and who was a very good friend, performed that ordination.

The twins graduated from eighth grade at the Riverside School in June 1914. They purchased class pins, shaped like a shield with gold trimmings, the face of the shield being red and green, the school colors. Mark wore his class pin for a number of years afterward, including during the time he was on his mission.

Mona and Mark went to the new West High School in the fall of 1914 just before their fourteenth birthday. Up until that time, these buildings were called the Salt Lake High School. But the East High School was completed that year, so Salt Lake City had for the first time both a West and an East High School.

*Mark in his West High
School band uniform,
1915*

Cadet work, or military training, was the vogue at the
school for all of the first- and second-year male students.
When the first day of drill was called, all male freshmen assembled on the campus. Captain Webb, a National Guard
officer, called for volunteers for the trumpet and drum
corps. Not knowing the first thing about either a drum or a
trumpet but hoping to escape the necessity of shouldering a
rifle in the drill, Mark stepped forward. He wished to be a
drummer, so a drummer he became. He bought a second-
hand drum at the Beesley Music Company and started the
painful job of learning to play under the tutelage of Wayne
Corbus, an older high school student.

Considerable interest was developed in the cadet organization of both high schools by the promise of a trip to the San
Francisco World's Fair in 1915. It seemed a great idea until
spring came, and with it the realization that the cadets personally would have to dig up enough money to pay their

Mark as a teenager

transportation and other expenses. Then it was a different story. Mark remembered that Captain Webb and George Eaton, the principal, came to his home one night at supper-time and arranged with his father to allow him to go to California with the cadets.

The band made the trip that summer and was gone five weeks. They visited San Francisco for ten days, Los Angeles for several days, San Diego, where the Panama Pacific Exposition was being held, for a week, and various other places. The drummers had a rough time in San Francisco, for the fog dampened the heads of the drums so that the instruments sounded like Indian drums, much to the disgust of Captain Webb. It was hardly military-like, he thought, to have a battalion of cadets march down Market Street to the sound of tom-toms.

All during the four years at West High School, Mark carried paper routes for the *Salt Lake Telegram*. During this

time the *Salt Lake Herald Republican,* a morning paper
owned by President Heber J. Grant, went out of business,
and the *Telegram* attempted to publish both morning and
evening papers. Mark carried both papers until the arrange-
ment failed and the *Telegram* continued publication as an
evening and Sunday morning paper. His brother Claude assisted on Sundays when he had a heavy load, and they delivered the papers in a little red wagon, one of them pulling the
wagon while the other took the papers to the porches.

By this time Christian was constructing houses and selling them as a business. He built a large bungalow at 848 East
6th South in 1917, but the people who bought it were not
able to keep up their payments. They asked permission to be
released from the contract. Instead of reselling the house,
Christine persuaded her husband to let their family move
into it.

At the time they made the move, Mark was only seventeen years of age, but Bishop Kershaw N. White of the 26th
Ward felt the young man should be ordained an elder. He
made the necessary arrangements with the stake presidency,
and the ordination took place in the 26th Ward on June 16,
1918, performed by Ernest Karl Janke.

In the fall of 1918, Mark entered the University of Utah.
Classes began in September, but within two or three weeks
the great influenza epidemic of 1918-19 occurred, and all
schools and churches were closed. As soon as the university
was reopened the next spring, Mark returned to his classes.

On February 5, 1919, he obtained his endowments in the
Salt Lake Temple. He learned to love the temple from that
time and began attending it quite regularly, spending nearly
every Monday there. On one of these occasions a sharp
earthquake occurred in the Salt Lake Valley. Mark was sitting
in the Terrestrial Room at the time. There was no damage to
the temple, but he was awed to hear that big building actually
groan as it resisted the shaking of the earthquake.

In their new home, the Petersens were members of the
First Ward of Liberty Stake. When Mona and Mark attended

Sunday School there for the first time, Bishop John C. Duncan met them at the door and asked most cordially if they were a newly married couple.

At this Sunday School Mark caught his first glimpse of the girl who was to become his wife, Emma Marr McDonald, the Sunday School organist. Mark's early acquaintanceship with Emma Marr was rather interesting, to him at least. Although he saw her several times in the ward, the first occasion where they were formally introduced was following a chorus practice in the LeGrand Ward, where a group had gone to rehearse for a program to be given in the Salt Lake Tabernacle.

Mark's first close association with Emma Marr came during the spring of 1919, when he began leading the ward choir and she played the organ. He was not a musician and had not been trained to lead singing, but because he had a fair singing voice, he was pressed to lead the choir. Emma Marr discovered immediately, as a musician herself, that not only was he unable to lead properly, but he couldn't even beat time. So she greatly disliked his directorship. But Willis J. Woodbury, who would become one of Mark's and Emma's closest friends, saved the day. He taught Mark how to wield the baton.

"Although Emma Marr at first resisted my efforts at being a choir leader," Mark wrote in his life story, "after the first month or so she literally put me over as such. She was in large measure responsible for the success that attended our efforts to present a musical program consisting of selections from Evan Stephens's pen, with orchestra accompaniment, for the dedication of the First Ward chapel in 1919. President Heber J. Grant dedicated the chapel. After that, our association became very interesting to me—cordial, but in no wise intimate. I spent several evenings with her and we went to theaters together a few times. The association up to this period was really merely friendship. Then I was called on a mission."

The letter from Box B reached Mark just about Christmastime in 1919. He was to leave in mid-January. Although

Mark had indicated a preference for Denmark, the call was to Eastern Canada, with Toronto, Ontario, as the headquarters. Due to unsettled post-war conditions, no elders were then being sent to Europe.

What money Mark could scrape together was used for the mission, and Claude and his father supplied the rest of the expense. The ward choir, of which he was still director, held a little party for him on the amusement-hall stage at the ward the week before his departure and presented him with a small copy of the Doctrine and Covenants and a hymnbook, both fine volumes bound in morocco leather. The Sunday School class that Mark taught (and in which President Gordon B. Hinckley was then a boyhood member) gave him a copy of the Book of Mormon.

"My farewell testimonial for the mission was on January 14, 1920, the Monday preceding my departure. As I looked back at it now, it was quite a coincidence that Jessie Evans, who later became Jessie Evans Smith, the wife of President Joesph Fielding Smith, provided most of the music for my farewell. The coincidence occurred in that it was Joseph Fielding Smith who set me apart for my mission. In later years they became our intimate friends. Jessie Evans was a very close friend of Emma Marr, and they engaged in musical activities together over a period of years.

"Most of the crowd attending the farewell was made up of people from the 26th Ward and swelled the congregation to the extent that the hall could hardly contain them."

3

The McDonalds

"I will bring you to Zion"
(Jeremiah 3:14)

In order to understand the role Emma Marr McDonald and her mother, Sarah McDiarmid McDonald, played in Mark's mission, a look at the events leading up to their joining the Church is important.

Emma Marr was born in Sydney, Nova Scotia, Canada, to John Alexander McDonald and Sarah McDiarmid, both of whose parents had immigrated from the highlands of Scotland to Nova Scotia. Her father was a sailing-ship captain, her mother a schoolteacher. About six months before Emma was born, her parents and her brother, Jack, were traveling from Glace Bay, Cape Breton, Nova Scotia, to St. John, Newfoundland, aboard the sailing ship *Emma Marr*. An explosion occurred in the hold of the ship, tearing a huge hole in the side of the vessel. All hands took to the lifeboats, and inside half an hour the *Emma Marr* sank. During their time in the lifeboats, the crew was ordered by Sarah to sing hymns loudly. Rough sailors had no interest in religious songs, but Sarah McDonald commanded respect and obedience then and throughout her life. They all sang until they were hoarse, principally the Salvation Army song "Pull for the Shore." After spending ten hours in a rough sea clad only in their nightclothes, the entire crew and the captain's family were rescued.

When Emma was born, her parents decided to name her after the lost vessel, so she was christened Emma Marr in the Presbyterian faith. The Reverend Mr. Rankin officiated. Her father, Captain John, became the captain of the sailing ship

Paramatta at that time, and for four years the family sailed wherever the *Paramatta* took them.

In Ireland a young goat was acquired to supply fresh milk, becoming a dear pet as well. Throughout her life Emma Marr retained a fascination for goats, pictures of goats, stories about goats, and especially songs relating to goats. Her earliest recollection of shipboard life was of an old seaman lifting her up on a table to cut her toenails. Before she was three years old, she had crossed the Atlantic Ocean six times as well as made other long voyages. But when her brother, Jack, became of school age, the family's roving life had to be abandoned.

At this time the old sailing ships were gradually being replaced by steamers. Captain John, a handsome, black-haired intellectual with a Van Dyke beard, realized the situation and decided that he must update his training. In order to qualify as a steamship captain, it was necessary to pass examinations to obtain a certificate or ticket, as it was called. This meant the dashing captain must start over as a junior officer on a steamship and work his way up. The family moved to Liverpool, England, where this was accomplished. Emma Marr was four years old.

Because she was very precocious, Emma Marr was placed immediately in a private school in Liverpool kept by two highly educated but somewhat ancient maiden ladies of Scottish extraction. Here her troubles began. Indulged by captain and crew, she had sailed for the first four years of her life. Now her adored father was away for six months at a time, and her mother, raised in the old school, which stressed the importance of the sons of the family, seemed to spend all her time with Jack. Sarah was concerned that with the absence of Captain John, Jack's development would be in some way damaged, so she tried to be both mother and father to the boy. Emma Marr should, like all young girls, play with her dolls and take care of herself.

Sarah had been raised in the strictest Scottish Presbyterian tradition in a remote Canadian settlement. She *knew* how little girls should be dressed, and she clothed Emma Marr accordingly. But the primitive frocks, underwear, and stockings that the child wore to school caused uncontrollable mirth among her schoolmates. Emma Marr never forgot her humiliation as the girls in her class pulled at her clothing, pointing and laughing and calling names.

To add to her confusion, Emma Marr was the center of her father's world. When he was in Liverpool, she was showered with gifts of toys and clothing in the latest fashion. Her father couldn't spend enough time with her; she was his princess. But as soon as Captain John sailed away, the fancy dresses disappeared and again she became the brunt of jokes, clothed in the manner of a proper backwoods Presbyterian child.

The Misses Donaldson, who ran her school, expected super achievements from the dark-haired Emma with the astonishing blue eyes.

In recalling her unhappy days with the Misses Donaldson, Emma wrote: "The younger of the sisters at once impressed me with her fierceness of manner. She wore two pairs of glasses at once and looked over the rims of both, seldom if ever through the lens. Her struggles to keep her false teeth in place were apparent to all. This filled me with a sensation of awe and amazement. The older one was more restrained in manner, but a certain tightening of the lips made me suspect that she was the fiercer of the two. I was a very cowardly child, having never been away from my parents before in my life, and spending every day with total strangers was, I think, one of my most terrifying experiences. Of course, I was more or less a curiosity among the other scholars, who made no attempt to conceal their amusement at my odd clothes and still odder speech gleaned from constant association with sailors. This may have been the cause of the inferiority complex that still troubles me.

"There were other teachers at the school, a Mr. Hodgson, who taught singing, and one or two others. The only thing that I enjoyed at all was the crowing of the cuckoo clock that told how near it was to going-home time. With the change in my father's position, we did not have as much money, and Miss Donaldson's school was expensive as well as exclusive, so my mother transferred me to another private school that was larger and cheaper, kept by a Miss Mary Fairgleave. My brother attended a church school where, unlike myself, he did excellent work right from the start. In his last year he won a four-year scholarship to attend technical school with all expenses paid, his books supplied, and a generous bonus as well. During this particular period my main interest was swimming."

In this period of unhappiness for Emma Marr, seemingly her only pleasure at school was competitive swimming, and she won many medals. Their mother thought it proper that Jack receive piano lessons. From the time she was tiny, Emma Marr had been able to hum accurately any tune she heard only once. Now as the dignified old teacher with his portfolio and his pince-nez came weekly to teach Jack, Emma always devised ways to be within listening distance of his lectures. Jack hated piano lessons—he wanted to go outside and play football. But in the early 1900s when the males of the family were given all the advantages, it never occurred to the McDonalds to teach their gifted daughter instead of her uninterested brother. Emma spent many hours standing behind the gold velvet drapes in the music room, drinking in every word of Jack's "Herr Professor." As soon as he had departed for his next unwilling pupil, Emma Marr sat at the piano and played by ear the music she had heard the teacher play. Painfully, she taught herself to read music. Soon her sight-reading skills equaled her ability to play by ear. And she discovered that she could easily transpose any composition into any key. At long last her music gave her enormous satisfaction and the emotional release that had been absent from her life.

During the Boer War with England, the ship on which Captain John sailed was drafted into military service as a prison ship. He was away for some eight months, and on his return he regaled his family with stories of the war. Captain

John was promoted regularly, and when he again attained
the rank of captain, he was given command of the steamship
Virginian, an old though quite large steamer sailing to Hull,
England; Antwerp, Belgium; and Montreal, Canada. As his
ship did not call at Liverpool, his family frequently went to
one of his ports of call and stayed with him on board the
ship, nearly always at Hull, occasionally at Antwerp, and Jack
once sailed with him to Montreal under an assumed name so
no one would know he was the son of the captain. The Captain had a lot of bad luck with the *Virginian.* After one particularly violent storm in which the anchor was lost and the
ship damaged considerably, he thought he was in danger of
being demoted. Instead of this, he was given a smaller although much newer and finer ship, sailing between London,
England, and Havana, Cuba.

During one of Captain John's lengthy voyages, two Mormon missionaries called at the McDonald house in Liverpool
to see a Mr. Wallace, another seafaring man who had stayed
with them for a time. They then lived at No. 10 Oriel Road in
Boodle, a suburb of Liverpool. Sarah, mostly on account of
their unusual American accent, made the missionaries welcome. After several visits still in the pursuit of Mr. Wallace, or
at least using him as an excuse, the elders delivered their
message to Sarah. The young men were fresh-faced, honest,
and appealing. Sarah, raised a devout Presbyterian, knew her
Bible backward and forward, better than the elders. A
schoolteacher and a student of many subjects, she could find
no contradiction in the gospel as presented by these enthusiastic young missionaries. Excitement filled her soul as
she considered the possibilities of a pre-earth life as a child
of God.

A steady steam of elders came to No. 10 Oriel Road. Evenings were pleasant with gospel conversations, Emma's
music, and good food. One of the elders was John C. Duncan
(who was later bishop of the First Ward when the Petersen
family moved to 848 East Sixth South). His bright mind and
solid testimony served to reinforce the strong belief growing

in Sarah's soul. Finally, most thrilling of all, Heber J. Grant
began calling on the McDonald family in his capacity as mission president. Great gospel discussions lasting long into the
night became a nucleus not only for Sarah's testimony but
also a close friendship that lasted until President Grant's
death. For years after he became President of the Church,
Heber J. Grant took Sarah McDonald on long automobile
rides and recalled those early days in Liverpool. Her
thorough knowledge of the Bible and devotion to scripture
reading were to make her a powerful advocate of the Lord
Jesus Christ and His restored church.

Emma Marr and Jack enjoyed their association with the
elders and the social life thus brought to their home. They
too had been schooled in the scriptures in the Presbyterian
Church. Their testimonies of the truth grew until their desire
for baptism equaled that of their mother.

When Captain John returned from the Boer War, he discovered that his wife and children had been spending their
time with the Mormons. He was not nearly as jubilant about
the message of the new gospel as was his family. As he con-
sulted with various ministers and questioned the reputation
of the elders and their church, his attitude became still less
favorable, and at last he forbade his family either to attend
meetings or to receive visits from the elders or other members of the Mormon church. Then he left on another voyage.

Sarah McDonald could not live without the gospel of
Jesus Christ, so she decided to continue her association with
the Church. It was not in a spirit of deception that she and
her children attended meetings and welcomed the elders
into their home. They sincerely believed that in time the
truth of the gospel would be manifest to Captain John.

Emma recalled, "Our meetings with the elders and Saints
were necessarily clandestine, but nevertheless the intimacy
grew rapidly. One most uncomfortable episode stands out
clearly in memory. My father's ship usually sailed Saturday
afternoon, and this time he left as usual Saturday morning.
The following day was Liverpool conference, held in

Burnley, and Mother left late Saturday night to be there bright and early for the morning meetings. When she returned home, she discovered that my Dad's ship had missed the tide and he had returned home to find his wife away and his son and daughter fibbing bravely to try to account for her all-night absence in some logical way.

"My father was the soul of generosity, and nothing was ever denied us that it was possible for him to provide. It was a hard blow to his pride that we wanted to join such an unpopular, ill-spoken-of sect. He suffered terribly over the whole affair, being forced by his profession to leave home and not knowing what his family would do the moment his back was turned. The more I think about it, the more I understand his point of view.

"One night in a particularly quarrelsome mood, he told my mother to go ahead and join the Mormons. So at the first opportunity she took him at his word and was baptized by Elder John C. Duncan, who remained her friend for the rest of her life."

One summer during school vacation, Captain John asked Sarah if she and Emma would like to take a trip to Cape Breton, Nova Scotia, to visit relatives. They were both delighted at the prospect. The line for which he now sailed had a rule that none of their captains could allow any member of his family to travel on his ship, so Sarah and Emma sailed from Liverpool the same day that Captain John's vessel left London for Boston. The two ships arrived in Boston within an hour of each other. There the family were guests at the home of Stanton King, the manager of the Sailor's Haven. From Boston, mother and daughter sailed to Halifax, and on that short trip Emma had her first and last bout with seasickness.

After Sarah and Emma had visited with their Cape Breton relatives for a month, Sarah received a letter from Captain John in which he made the astonishing declaration that if she would not agree to sever all connections and communications with the Mormons, she need expect no further financial support from him. He knew that because of his captaincy on

steamships, the family had become accustomed to a reason-
able amount of luxury, including several servants in their
home. Sarah had not been in good health, so she could not
obtain employment. Thus Captain John thought his family
would be forced to renounce their religion, as they would
have no means of earning a livelihood, Emma being too
young and Sarah not well enough to work. They discovered
later that it was at the suggestion of their former Presbyterian
minister that this letter was written. Emma never saw her
father again. She was fifteen years old.

Sarah obtained a position for her daughter as a clerk in a
dry-goods store at three dollars a week. Her duties consisted
of helping to sell laces and ribbons when an extra clerk was
needed, and otherwise doing odd jobs. She remembered
taking home, one at a time, three stuffed white baby seals to
clean with cornmeal. Emma was the special assistant of the
junior member of the firm of McCurdy and Company. After
she had been there only a few months, she was promoted to
the position of cashier, a nerve-racking job for a very young
girl. Later a friend, Margaret Gardner, married, and Emma
got her job as a bookkeeper in the firm of Kirk and Torey,
Importers. Jack joined his mother and sister in Sydney as
soon as he could get across the ocean. He obtained employment at once at the Nova Scotia Iron and Steel plant.

When Emma first started to work, her mother's aunt Mary
McRae let them have a room in her large house on the
Esplanade. She had a motley assortment of boarders and
roomers, some sober, the majority not. Sarah and Emma
rented the downstairs front room with the telephone in it,
and against their will they managed to hear everybody's business. Outstanding in their memory of those days was the
one-eyed evil-looking gray tomcat that was almost as big as
an Airedale terrier; the deaf mute who once made advances
to Dolena, the young daughter of the house, who decorated
him with a swiftly and expertly thrown plate of butter she
happened to be carrying at the time; Mr. Sutherland, a mild-
mannered fellow of quiet demeanor when he was sober,

which was perhaps three-fourths of the time, but a holy ter-
ror under the influence; and his bosom companion, Paddy
Haley, a loafing, laughing, lying Irishman who had an elegant
tongue in his head. A frequent visitor to the house was one
James McLean (who would play an important role in Mark
Petersen's mission a few years later).

As soon as they could afford it after Jack arrived, the family rented the two upper floors of a house next door to Aunt
Mary's place. A Jewish rabbi, Sakuta, and his family lived on
the ground floor. On coming home one night, the rabbi
found Mrs. Sakuta totally bereft of her powers of speech,
owing to the shock of hearing the tramp of heavy feet all over
the house at a time when no one else was home. The structure had originally been built three miles up Sydney River.
An unusually brutal murder had been committed there, and
it had the reputation of being haunted. After it had been va-
cant for a long time, the landlord decided to move it to town
in an effort to rent it, though he himself refused to live in it.
But at least the haunted house sheltered the McDonalds until
they found an apartment that suited them better.

Had Emma but known, during almost any part of her stay
in Canada, she might have demanded an increase of salary
for drawing people to the places where she worked—so
great was the curiosity of people to see a real live Mormon
girl.

There were no Mormon missionaries within six hundred
miles of Sydney, so the McDonalds used to pay tithing regularly to conference headquarters at Portland, Maine. Three
times during their stay they were visited by elders. One of
them was Warren Colton, who baptized Emma one warm
summer night in Sydney harbor.

"After my baptism, religious persecution increased
against us," she wrote. "Jack moved westward to the big steel
mills at Gary, Indiana, but Mother and I remained in Sydney.
Because there was no Mormon congregation and we were
churchgoing people, we regularly attended the Presbyterian
church in Sydney. I had been asked to be organist for the

Sarah McDonald, front center, with Emma Marr (right), son Jack (center), and Jack's wife, Donna (left); Captain John McDonald, inset. Because the McDonalds left England quickly and without prior preparation, no photos are available of Emma at an earlier age

congregation and joyfully played for their services. One Sunday the minister had had his fill of the description of my baptism in Sydney harbor, which had become a much-talked-of event. He stood at the pulpit and, raising his arm, pointed to Mother and me, exclaiming that in the congregation there were two enemies of God who had been seduced by an evil sect. He ordered his flock to stop speaking to us, to refuse to sell us food or clothing, and to regard our presence as if we represented the devil. Soon it became so uncomfortable in Sydney that when Bishop Duncan wrote offering to lend us money for fare to Salt Lake City, we eagerly accepted."

When Sarah and Emma Marr McDonald arrived in Zion, Bishop Duncan and his wife offered every kindness imaginable. They opened their home to the weary travelers, and

Jack too, when he joined them, welcoming them into their own family until the three could obtain employment.

The first Sunday in Salt Lake City, Emma was called from the congregation to substitute for the regular pianist, who had failed to arrive. The meeting was held in the basement because the building was still under construction and the chapel was not yet completed. Emma Marr's adult height was only five feet. A straight-backed chair too low for comfort had been pulled up to the piano. She spied a large Bible on the stand and appropriated the book to give her the height she needed in order to see the conductor. Later in the meeting, when the speaker wanted to quote from the scriptures and began looking for the Bible, a titter of amusement went over the congregation because it was very apparent that Emma was sitting on the Good Book.

Frank Penrose of the Presiding Bishop's Office found Emma a job as a bookkeeper. Sarah became a hotel maid. When the United States entered the first world war, Jack was one of the first men drafted from Salt Lake City. This placed most of the burden for financing the McDonald home upon Emma Marr. Finally, at the suggestion of D. Ray Shurtliff, who had been a missionary in England during the time of the McDonalds' conversion, Emma applied for a position as bookkeeper at the Salt Lake Knitting Works. She was hired at eighty-five dollars a month, an increase of twenty dollars over her last employment.

4

The Mission

"The field is white already to harvest"
(D&C 4:4)

When the 5:15 P.M. train left Salt Lake City Wednesday afternoon, January 14, 1920, it carried a large company of missionaries, including four elders bound for Canada. Mark had purchased his ticket, but with no previous travel experience, he had neglected to buy a Pullman berth. The future world traveler enjoyed seeing the Mississippi River for the first time, as well as the mills and elevators of the Quaker Oats company at Cedar Rapids, Iowa.

After two days and nights, the train pulled into Chicago— in Mark's words, "The noisiest place I have ever been yet." A platoon of old-fashioned cabs met the elders and carried them to the Majestic Hotel, where space had been reserved by the Church. The four missionaries spent the evening "writing cards and letters to most everyone we knew."

Arrival at their destination seemed the least of the elders' problems, and the next morning Mark left for Detroit to spend a week with his brother Chris while the others saw the Chicago sights. Mark had wired his arrival time to his brother, but no one met the train. The young elder, after waiting a long and disappointing two hours, found a hotel and went to bed. The next day he asked directions to Rochester, where Chris and his family lived on a small farm. An interurban train went to the Detroit suburb, and a taxi deposited Mark on Chris's doorstep. He rang the bell, which was answered by his brother, who "didn't know me from Adam." Mark asked if this were the Christian Petersen residence. On receiving an affirmative reply, he blurted, "Well, I'm your little brother." When Chris had left home, Mark was still in short pants.

After a week's visit, a highlight of which was a tour of the Ford plant in Detroit where Chris worked, Mark boarded a train for Niagara Falls. Parts of the falls were frozen, and Mark walked around and on them before catching a train for his mission headquarters at Toronto. At the customs office at the border, the missionary was denied admittance into Canada, given deportation papers with a ticket to the United States, and sent back on a train to the American side. In his own words, "I was angry enough to chew nails."

Angry he was. Discouraged he was not. He took a train to Buffalo that night, slept in the depot, and in the morning boarded another train for Toronto. This time he made it. After a much-needed bath, he joined President Nephi Jensen for dinner and discovered that another of the four elders, not a citizen of the United States, had been turned back. Mark felt convinced that only the help of the Lord allowed him across the border the second time he tried.

At a five-hour priesthood meeting, four elders, including Mark, were assigned to reopen the Nova Scotia Conference, which had been closed for twenty years. En route they stopped in Montreal for sightseeing. In St. Johns, New Brunswick, they visited with local elders and inspected places of interest. After four days they arrived in Halifax and found a room.

Permission to preach was necessary before tracting or any other activities could be initiated. At a meeting of the Halifax Privileges Committee, the elders were queried extensively about polygamy and asked to write a repudiation of this doctrine. Mark discovered that it was easier for him to express himself in writing than any of the others, so he was appointed scribe for the period of his mission.

After several days of enforced inactivity alleviated only by scriptural study among themselves (Mark called it "watchful waiting"), the elders appeared before the city council on Friday, February 21, 1920. Without a hearing, the elders' petition and Mark's letter repudiating polygamy were read aloud, followed by a blistering letter from the most prominent minister in Halifax. This cleric wrote that it would be "a grave mistake on the part of the Council to allow the Mormon Society any privilege whatsoever, for it mattered not what they said before permission was given to preach publicly, but after permission had been granted, they might begin preaching to this respectable city the abominable doctrines that had been cried down in the United States."

One alderman moved that the elders not be granted their petition. Another rose and said that if "four men began preaching here, it would not be long until a goodly congregation was converted and in time would increase to the extent that they would gain control of the city parliament and establish laws permitting plural marriage, a doctrine abominable in the sight of the world, yet believed by the Mormons." The motion was seconded and carried. It was a polite invitation to move out of town. The next petition was from a man who wanted to open a pool hall in the city. Immediately he was granted permission. Four discouraged elders wired President Jensen for instructions.

Mark wrote in his journal: "Saturday, February 21, is a blue day for all of us. We don't KNOW what to do. I arose feeling fine and read a while. The other brethren did not feel very good and I soon caught their spirit. I didn't even shave this morning. We are waiting instructions from the president. I have received no mail for a week and a half."

The following Thursday marked two happy events—the arrival of President Jensen to appeal to the Halifax City Council, and a letter from Sister Sarah McDonald of the First Ward with the names of Mr. and Mrs. Fred Hollands and Mr. and Mrs. James McLean.

President Jensen appeared before the Deputy Mayor of Halifax, who offered a kind of apology for the council's treatment of the elders. He said that in order to maintain the old

Two photographs taken of Mark while he was on his mission

tradition that the Union Jack stood for free speech, the officials would allow the elders to work in their city. But the elders were in nowise welcome, and it was hoped that the good people would not be deceived and would realize that the Mormons were not wanted in Halifax. Two of the elders crossed the bay to Dartmouth, where they were treated with kindness. There should be no trouble getting to work in Dartmouth.

Mark recorded, "On Sunday, February 29, we found our first friend, a personal friend of Sister Sarah McDonald, a Mr. James McLean. We visited with him and his family and were treated royally. He offered his home for cottage meetings. We thanked God most heartily for this good fortune."

Finally, after two months of discouraging delays, the elders hired a hall and began tracting the city of Halifax. Twenty-five investigators came to their first meeting on Sunday, March 7, 1920. Unfortunately, the custodian with the keys to the building was not among them. After waiting in the cold for almost an hour, the elders passed out pamphlets and invited the group to return the following Sunday. In his journal Mark exclaimed, "O death—where is thy sting!"

The results of years of scriptural study begin to reveal themselves as Mark describes his conversations while tracting. His strong belief that converts must be taken from the known to the unknown—from the Bible, which a compassionate Father has placed in almost every home, to the Book of Mormon brought by the elders—finds its foundations in his mission experience. Each of the four elders in Halifax seems to have gone tracting on his own. Mark discovered that if his door approach mentioned the Bible, fewer doors slammed in his face. What respectable citizen of the fair city of Halifax would deny a belief in the Good Book?

With his Bible, Mark proved that the apostasy began during the life of Christ. Still from the Bible he read of the Restoration, the restitution of all things that would occur in modern times in the hour of God's judgment. Then, asking his contact if he knew the signs by which this modern restored church could be recognized, he ticked off Ephesians 4, Hebrews 5, Exodus 28, Acts 13, Amos 3:7, and, for a grand finale, Isaiah 29:11-14 and Ezekiel 37. Later in life his insistence on teaching the milk before the meat and his conviction that conversion should rest on the Bible before the Book of Mormon resulted from this early tracting. His emphasis on quality baptisms, "that your fruit should remain," began in Halifax in 1920. This belief finally led him to type pertinent passages from the Old Testament and the Book of Mormon onto onionskin paper and glue them into a small New Testament that fit into his suit pocket. He claimed that his little book held all the information needed for true conversion. He preached from this small volume and allowed few to examine his "life's work." His cross-references predated the Church's editions of the scriptures published some sixty years later.

Stories of the great Halifax explosion fascinated the elders. Two ships, one filled with gun powder, had collided in the harbor during World War I. Flames from the resulting explosion burned half of Halifax and caused great physical injury to the population. Whenever the Mormon missionaries contacted someone who had difficulty understanding their message, they wondered if the person's ears had been injured by the Halifax explosion.

His companion was Elder Baker, "the most cheerful man I think I ever met—frecklefaced with a broad smile. And when he would walk up to a door, the people would smile back immediately. They were very respectful of him, too, because he was over six feet tall and weighed 250 pounds. Nobody argued very much with Elder Baker."

The work in Halifax settled into a routine with tracting all day, cottage meetings in the evening, generally at the McLeans', study early and late, and hall meetings on Sunday. Quotes from Mark's journal include these:

"I distributed 237 tracts today and noticed a keen appetite tonight." "I saw a streetcar jump the tracks and turn halfway around crossways on the street, and I finished another straight reading of the Book of Mormon." "We had a great treat tonight and saw the northern lights for the first time in our lives." "Some cats fought on the fence below our windows and we threw nearly everything but our Bibles at them, one of the brethren suggesting that we might need them sometime." "Today I received a letter with a dollar bill in it." "I tracted in fog so dense and wet that it fell in tiny drops of water to the ground and settled on my clothes like heavy dew." "I met two people who believed in the Bible only when the lid was closed and refused to listen to the words which I read to them." "I enjoy my work but am weak and must be humble and put my trust in the Lord." "I found a man who believed strongly in infant baptism. When he couldn't find a scripture to substantiate his argument and I pressed him, he became very angry and escorted me to the door of his shop with a hammer in his hand."

On Sunday, June 6, 1920, Mark had his first experience
with the power of inspiration. He had enthusiastically begun
a sermon when suddenly he felt weak and entirely alone. He
groped for words, his mind a blank. He knew that the Spirit
had left him. He attempted to finish his talk but failed miser-
ably. "Then I knew what it meant to be in tune with the
Spirit," he wrote, "and I knew how it felt to be out of tune
with the Spirit. From now on I will depend more upon God
and less upon myself."

Occasionally humorous experiences brightened the
work. One morning while tracting, Mark knocked on a door
and introduced himself as a Mormon missionary. Angrily, the
woman of the house shouted, "When you people stop mas-
sacring the Armenians will be time enough to come around
doing missionary work." Mark had to explain that he was a
Mormon, not a Mohammedan.

Elder Baker and Mark were sent to the little town of
Windsor on July 20 to tract, rent a hall, and generally open
the work. They were astonished to find the bay bone dry at
low tide but forty feet deep at high tide. Windsor was surrounded by rich farmlands. The two elders called on local
ministers to introduce themselves and assure the clerics of
their good intentions. Mark recalls, "I never before in my life
had quite such a successful day. The Spirit of the Lord was
with us most abundantly. Each minister we called on almost
melted in front of us. My testimony grows every day, and I
thank God from the bottom of my heart that I am here and
will do my best to help the good work along regardless of the
costs."

Hoping that July 24 would bless their pioneering effort,
the elders held their first open-air meeting in Windsor. Following a Salvation Army gathering, they jumped up and
started speaking before the crowd could disperse. Elder
Baker began, then Mark spoke for almost an hour. One
hundred people remained in their seats. The Mormons concluded with the hymn "Israel, Israel, God Is Calling" and
passed out tracts.

Elder Baker was a monotone. Mark felt convinced that this unfortunate condition could be overcome with a little diligent work. So every evening after dinner, the two elders went out into the woods on the edge of town and practiced singing. Their repertoire consisted of three hymns, which they sang until dark. One day on a downtown street a man called to them, "Hello, boys. Why don't you go out in the woods and have a song?"

As the Mormon meetings in Windsor began to attract more than fifty people each Sunday night, the initial friendliness of the clergymen was withdrawn. Mark was amazed to read in the weekly paper distorted quotations from B. H. Roberts and the Doctrine and Covenants. The mayor withdrew permission to hold street meetings. The friendly smiles that had been the rule as the missionaries walked down the street were replaced by sneering faces and pointing fingers. The elders decided it was time to tract the nearby village of Wentworth.

When every house in both Windsor and Wentworth had been contacted at least once, President Boyack, head of the conference, recalled the missionaries and suggested that they might work Halifax during the week and return to Windsor for the Sunday meetings. It was at this time that Mark found Mr. and Mrs. Whidden Shaw, who believed his message and treated him with kindness. The Shaws were not baptized for another year, but Mrs. Shaw continued to write Mark, asking gospel questions and telling of their experiences. After his return to Halifax Mark received the following song from her, paraphrased from a Presbyterian hymn:

Standing by a purpose true, heeding God's command,
Honor them the faithful few; all hail the Mormon band.
Dare to be a Mormon, dare to stand alone;
Dare to have a purpose firm, dare to make it known.

Many mighty men are lost daring not to stand,
Who for God had been a host by joining the Mormon band.

Many giants great and tall stalking through the land,
Headlong to the earth would fall if met by the Mormon band.

Hold the Gospel banner high on the victory ground,
Satan and his host defy and shout for the Mormon band.
Dare to be a Mormon, dare to stand alone;
Dare to have a purpose firm, dare to make it known.

After reading Mrs. Shaw's letter, Mark wrote in his journal, "Mrs. Shaw, I think, will soon accept the gospel."

The little song with its theme of courage in adversity sustained Mark on his mission and later whenever things seemed to go wrong. He truly believed that one must dare to be a Mormon and be prepared to stand alone when required to do so. He later referred to "Dare to Be a Mormon" in private conversations, in stake conferences, and from the Salt Lake Tabernacle pulpit.

5

Tracting and Teaching

"He reasoned with them out of the scriptures"
(Acts 17:2)

As his mission continued, Mark's enjoyment of speaking and writing knew no bounds. His journal is sprinkled with accounts of hour-long dissertations that were respectfully considered by his audiences. Some of these speeches he condensed and submitted to the local newspapers, where they were published. However, his literary taste was not always sublime, as can be gathered from the following words from his journal:

As the rain and sleet descended one dark and dreary night
We thought our days were ended when at last we saw a light.
We walked up to the window, saw a man with graying hair.
As we knocked he rose and shook his fist and then began to swear:
"You abominable, abominable Mormons, you're always in the
  way;
You come to get my daughter and coax my wife away.
I'll just unchain my watchdog and see what he can do."
But to save all this bad trouble, we took our grips and flew.

On Thursday, September 16, 1920, he noted, "I received a letter from home this morning which came on the first airship to enter Salt Lake on air duty. The envelope was stamped 'Received via air mail service. It took three days from Salt Lake to Halifax. Usually it takes a week."

The following Sunday, Mark again experienced the uncomfortable feeling of feeling absolutely on his own. With the vast fund of information that he continued to accumulate through long hours of study, he felt able to discuss most gospel subjects knowledgeably at length. Now he found that knowledge alone could not guarantee success. He was humbled and never forgot the lesson that he could preach only with the help of the Lord.

One day Mark and President Boyack appeared again before the Halifax officials, this time concerning permission to hold street meetings. While they waited their turn at the Metropolitan Hall, they sat through several hours of police court. For Mark, this experience planted the seed that grew to a great desire to be involved in newspaper work.

Then Mark and another elder were sent to Truro, where the atmosphere was so oppressive that tracting was difficult and depressing. One woman told Mark that someone should throw hot water on him for preaching Mormonism. Describing a street meeting where not one person stopped to listen, Mark concluded in his journal: "Oh rats!" However, the two elders continued contacting each home and business at least twice. In the entire town the elders neither received an invitation into a house nor heard a kind or considerate word. Mark noted, "Every place we go we get it in the neck. I nearly had a scrape with one man. If it hadn't been for my ministerial dignity, I believe I would have knocked him down."

He quoted from one newspaper account: "Beware the Mormons! Mormon missionaries are conducting a house-to-house canvass in this town in order to delude the people. We sincerely hope that no young person will be led away by these deceivers. Brigham Young in 1856 said when speaking of their ability to meet all opponents, 'We have the greatest and smoothest liars in the world.' He himself had 21 wives. Woman in Mormonism as in that crude Turkish religion Mohammedanism is reduced to be a mere serf and is denied any proper right or control of her mind and her body or her soul. There is no salvation for a woman and a woman is nothing in this Church. Mormonism therefore is the Islam of America, a fearless, slimy octopus reaching out its cruel tentacles to grip and strangle the moral life of the people. Let us then warn our young men and especially our young women of this terrible danger. One humorist hit it when he said that the Mormon religion is singular but their wives are plural."

Yet Mark somehow believed that Truro would someday become a thriving branch of the Church.

On November 6, three noteworthy events occurred. The first was the arrival of a birthday cake from Salt Lake City, one day before Mark's twentieth birthday. The two elders devoured it immediately. Next came a card from President Boyack instructing them that he thought it inadvisable for them to remain in Truro. They were to join two other elders in New Glasgow. And third, their bed broke. Mysteriously, Mark demolished three beds on his mission. This particular bed was repaired by the former carpenter, who just happened to have some nails in his pocket. Using a shoe and a Mentholatum jar as hammers, the two elders restored the bed to its former state, which lasted until they left for New Glasgow.

Due to the extremely cold weather, tracting in New Glasgow produced prodigious appetites. One evening as the four elders huddled near the fire, they decided that one of their number should go downtown to the grocery store to buy a coconut. The lot fell to Mark. Bundled against the arctic blast, he hurried down the street. To his surprise he saw a large Salvation Army street gathering in progress.

Although alone, he decided to hold a meeting immediately following the Salvation Army's. When the speaker recognized a Mormon elder in the audience, he immediately launched a tirade against the missionaries who teach of a Bible no one should believe. This served to rouse the interest of the crowd, which remained and listened with rapt attention as Mark preached the necessity of baptism. Meanwhile, fearing some accident, the other three elders began a search for their lost sheep and discovered Mark in the midst of one hundred interested listeners.

When New Glasgow was reopened, President Boyack, in tracting nearby Stellarton, discovered a seventy-three-year-old woman convert. She had given her heart and life to the gospel twenty-five years before and read from the Book of Mormon every day. For twenty years she had hidden her tithing money from her husband, who had neither interest in nor enthusiasm for the Church. When she discovered an elder on her doorstep, she asked him to wait, ran into her kitchen, and excitedly returned with a quarter century's honest tithe. Together the Murgatroyds welcomed the elders' visits. There the four elders spent their first Christmas away from home, cooking a traditional Christmas feast with a small substitution of roast pig for the turkey.

In New Glasgow, the missionaries met a family named Forrest. Mark wrote: "As we came to the door and knocked, the lady of the house invited us in immediately. She said, 'You're the gentlemen I have been expecting. But where is the book you are supposed to bring?' She explained that she had seen us both in a dream and identified us as we walked up the steps. We provided a Book of Mormon, and eventually the whole family was converted and remained faithful throughout their lives."

His first New Year's Day in the mission field brought Mark a deep sense of satisfaction. He felt that the previous 365 days had been the most profitable of his life. The year 1921 began with his renewed determination to "qualify myself for the work." He wanted to "do righteousness, preach righteousness, and to harm no person who might cross my way."

On January 8 Mark received another letter from Mrs. Shaw in which she bore strong testimony to the truth of the gospel. As yet she had not requested baptism. A trip to Halifax for a mission conference provided Mark and Elder Baker with an excuse to stop off in Windsor and visit the Shaw family, where "after the first two hours the conversation lagged, so we sang a few hymns which fit in very well." Poor Elder Baker could not escape singing so long as Mark was around.

The mission conference began with a record-breaking meeting, as five hundred investigators jammed every seat of

Acker's Theatre in Halifax. Mark sang in a missionary quartet, and President Jensen expounded for an hour and a half on the Mormon idea of hell. This was followed by a five-hour priesthood meeting.

Following the conference, Mark and Elder Baker stopped in Truro and drop-tracted the entire town before returning to New Glasgow. Mark could not overcome the feeling that although every home had been contacted and he had twice gone from one end of the village to the other, knocking on every single door without finding a friendly face, the possibility for Church membership was real. When as a member of the Council of the Twelve he toured the Nova Scotia Mission in 1981, he became misty-eyed as he visited Truro and saw a handsome Mormon meetinghouse in the little town.

In New Glasgow it became the custom for the four elders to go the the Murgatroyds' home on Saturday to do their washing and press their clothes for the Sabbath. They gladly made repairs needed by the elderly couple, including painting, wallpapering, building shelves, and repairing the plumbing. On Sundays they returned with food to cook for Sunday dinner. Still Mr. Murgatroyd refused to attend meetings or listen to the gospel message. But when the elders explained genealogy and prepared a Murgatroyd family tree, Mr. Murgatroyd participated enthusiastically. Mark suspected that the old man did not realize that genealogy was a religious subject.

Elder Baker had been supported on his mission by the rent from his Idaho farm. This money also provided for his wife and two small sons. Then the tall potato farmer received a letter telling of hardships at home and difficulties in collecting the rent and asking him to return home. Mark felt guilty that his mission seemed so easy compared to Elder Baker's. He wrote regretfully in his journal, "If the Lord had wanted Brother Baker out here any longer, He would have provided a way." Within a week, however, Elder Baker received a telegram from his wife stating that the problems at home had been settled and he should stay and fulfill his mis-

Missionaries of the Nova Scotia District, Eastern Canada Mission (Mark is standing, left)

sion. All the elders believed that divine intervention had allowed Elder Baker to remain in the field.

The New Glasgow newspaper editor accepted advertisments for local church meetings. When Mark and Elder Baker submitted a lengthy article and asked to pay for its publication, the editor offered to run it without charge. He also asked Mark to write a weekly column on Mormon beliefs.

While tracting, Mark met a man who had read the Book of Mormon but who discredited it by claiming that Joseph Smith must have been highly educated to translate it. Mark realized that his own knowledge of Joseph Smith was incomplete, and so he wrote home for all available information on the Prophet. This became a lifelong study until he felt as if he truly knew Joseph the Seer. Tracting also turned up two friendly old men, one of whom had subscribed to the *Salt Lake Tribune* for two years; the other had visited Salt Lake City and had mined in Park City. Mark expressed a universal missionary hope that someday he might have a baptism.

On February 21 Mark received a letter from Mrs. Shaw, expressing her desire to be baptized. She said she could hardly wait for spring to come so it would be warm enough to get in the water. Her husband had given up tobacco, and neither used tea. Each had finally "dared to be a Mormon and dared to stand alone!" A week later Mark received word that Elder Baker had been called home because of lack of funds. He would be accompanied to the United States by another elder who also was without financial support.

Mark's writing and preaching seem to have fallen into a pattern with weekly newspaper articles and ninety-minute sermons in the Sunday hall meetings. His journal entries reiterate his dependence upon the Lord: "I received some inspiration and for a while talking I had some ideas which had never occurred to me before." When he spoke at a Sunday meeting on "When Are We Saved?" he noted: "I don't know when I was blessed with a freer delivery or a clearer mind."

At another mission conference on April 30, Mark learned with some regret that he was to remain in Halifax with Elder Larsen, while Elders Boyack and Rentmeister were to travel in the country without purse or scrip. Early in May, Mark and Elder Larsen walked the first ten miles with Elders Boyack and Rentmeister and then watched as the companions, each with a grip in one hand and an umbrella in the other, disappeared down the dirt road. This left two lonely missionaries to labor in Halifax.

Mark prepared with extra care for his first Sunday meeting in Halifax. He was so sure of his talk that he forgot his earlier resolve to rely on the whisperings of the Spirit. Later he noted, "I attempted to preach and made the worst fizzle I have ever made of a sermon. I was totally devoid of the Spirit. I felt like some little schoolboy giving a recitation he had neglected to learn. It has been some time since I have been left so destitute by the Spirit that is promised to the elders as they preach. I shall try to study more and cultivate the Spirit during the week so that I will be better prepared next Sunday." The following Sunday he spoke on salvation for the dead and "was well blessed while doing so."

As temporary head of the Halifax Conference, Mark was

required to go through the mail. A request had come from a man in Logan, Utah, asking the elders to pursue some genealogical information. His mother, who had belonged to an aristocratic Halifax family, had paused in Salt Lake City en route to California. When she heard the teachings of the Latter-day Saints, so sure was she of the truth of these beliefs that she remained and became a schoolteacher in Salt Lake City. Later she met her husband and moved to Logan. Upon learning of her acceptance of Mormonism, her family disowned her, feeling that she had disgraced their honored name.

Mark decided to call on the woman's family in Halifax. Through the Halifax Probate Office he located an elderly gentleman, the lone survivor of the family there. Mark and Elder Larsen made an appointment for an evening visit. The old gentleman treated the elders with great cordiality until he discovered their religious affiliation. The thought of giving personal information to a Mormon seemed most abhorrent, and he expressed the firm opinion that the Mormons should be expelled from Nova Scotia. However, the diplomacy that dominated Mark's later life came to the fore, and eventually he obtained the information. As the elders left, the old man explained that he and his wife were already saved, and if they should die at that very moment, they "would be wafted into the presence of God and all His holy angels." Mark had come a long way from Salt Lake City.

Elders Boyack and Rentmeister returned from the country with stories of adventures that they told long into the night. Then, after Labor Day, it was Mark's and Elder Larsen's turn to go into the country without purse or scrip. They tracted Ingramport, Queensland, Hubbard's Cove, and finally East River—but were unsuccessful. At ten o'clock one night, tired and hungry, they found a kind elderly couple who fed them well and directed them to a gloriously soft bed with ropes under the mattress. Needless to say, the ropes broke at dawn. Mark wrote: "This makes the third bed we two have broken since we got together last September, and this is only June. What a reputation!" (Under the kind ministrations of the McLeans, the Shaws, and the Murgatroyds, Mark's 180 pounds swelled to 220 on his mission.)

The elders moved on to Lunenburg, a town of three thousand with a splendid harbor. Fishing schooners from the town traveled twice a year to Newfoundland, where they stayed until they were loaded with cod. Mark, curious and anxious to learn, watched the boats come in from their spring trip, filling the harbor with sailing vessels. On the wharves men dried the fish and put them into large warehouses, where the two elders saw more cod than they knew existed. They continued their march to Bridgewater, then to Hobbsville, where they attempted unsuccessfully to hire a hall. Tracting on, they began to find the houses far apart and the people unresponsive. To Midway and Italy Cross and on back to Bridgewater, the tired twosome trudged. Then both developed stomach flu, and as they had covered all the fishing villages on the schedule, they gratefully boarded a train for Halifax. Mark summarized his experience: "I am very glad to have been on this trip, where I have been humbled more than at any other time in my life."

President Jensen was due to arrive for a mission conference the end of July. The question in the minds of the elders was just how disappointed would he be when he discovered that there had been no baptisms. "We hold our breath in expectancy as we await his coming."

With President Jensen's arrival, Elder Boyack was released to return home, and Elder Lewis was appointed the new head of the Halifax Conference. Mark's new companion was Elder Leland Slater, who had arrived in the mission field just four weeks before. They were assigned to return to New Glasgow. Mark found that the same rooms where he had stayed the previous winter were available. The landlady welcomed the elders and immediately left them in charge of the house while she visited Vancouver, saying she would rather leave her home with the Mormon elders than with her own minister.

On August 1, a year and a half after the work was reopened

in Nova Scotia, the first baptisms took place near Halifax.
Brother and Sister Meeter, a couple who had read several
tracts and then sought out the elders, became the first new
members of the Church. The four New Glasgow elders celebrated the success with certainty that the work had been
launched at last.

Country tracting delighted the soul, if not the sole, and
Mark and Elder Slater began a canvass of the villages west of
New Glasgow. They covered thirty-two miles the first two
days, arriving at River John on August 26. Here Mark had the
first of many experiences of being healed while preaching,
yet with the affliction returning at the conclusion of his talk.
For three dollars the weary elders had rented a hall to hold
a meeting on Friday night. On Wednesday Mark felt ill but
tracted nevertheless. Thursday morning brought chills and
fever, which forced him to bed after several hours of work
that completed the tracting of the whole town. By noon Friday, Elder Slater, new to the field and feeling unable to
preach, gave Mark a very fervent blessing. Mark's chills and
fever continued to rage. At 6:30 Elder Slater helped Mark
dress and virtually carried him to the hall, where twenty
people waited. Mark had been praying throughout the day,
asking for strength to give the talk. He had prepared no sermon because of his illness, but the chills and fever vanished,
and he spoke for nearly an hour with great freedom. As soon
as he sat down, the illness returned.

Because of Mark's weakness, the two elders took a train
to their next stop, Pugwash, which they tracted in just six
hours. Elder Slater now joined Mark on the sick list. The next
village, Tatamagouche, although twenty-two miles away,
seemed an easy walk with gentle terrain and a cooling sea
breeze, so the weakened elders set out on foot on a two-day
journey. They quickly tracted Tatamagouche and decided to
walk toward River John. At each house along the way, the
people informed them that their minister had warned them
against the Mormons the previous Sunday. Finally, late in the
evening, the outline of a barn loomed in the distance. Stiff,

sore, tired, discouraged, weak in body but not in spirit, the two elders hobbled painfully to the barn, gathered some hay together, and lay down. The rising sun shed its light on the reason for their freezing night—frost sparkled everywhere.

Their tracting completed, Elder Slater and Mark left River John by train and returned to New Glasgow. Mark noted: "It was an invaluable experience for us, and we believe we helped the cause of truth so that it will be easier for the next elders who travel there." Waiting at Mark's flat was a sad letter from Mrs. Shaw explaining that although she was a Mormon in her heart, her husband refused his permission for her baptism. A note from the Halifax elders told of six baptisms to take place the following Sunday, four new members already baptized, and the hall meetings filled to overflowing.

By mid-October, the Sunday meetings at New Glasgow with Mark as principal speaker had dwindled from a high of only five in attendance to zero. But Mark had been shown a Catholic Bible for the first time in his life. So elated was he at discovering that he could prove the truth of Mormonism from this book that he felt no discouragement. His mind boggled at the possibilities of a new tool for the work. He discovered that the footnotes in the Catholic Bible were even more convincing for his case than the King James Version.

A mission conference on November 6, the day before he turned twenty-one, brought Mark back to Halifax, where he stopped to see the Shaws. Mr. Shaw's attitude had improved enormously, and he seemed to hang on every word Mark spoke. Mark wrote, "The Spirit of the Holy Ghost is now in their home. We felt it and enjoyed it."

The conference concentrated on the gifts of healing given to the elders. The four missionaries from New Glasgow returned home to find that Sister Murgatroyd had rented a new house and anxiously waited for them to move her and her things. They scrubbed the floors and windows, hung curtains, put down linoleum, arranged furniture, built a cupboard, and installed a door. Mark felt very happy with a hammer in his hands again.

On Thursday, December 22, the elders returned to Halifax for Christmas. All were curious about an Elder Whitehead who was receiving mail at the Halifax address but had not as yet made an appearance. Mark hoped this unknown elder was not his replacement. He had left home on January 14, so his two years would be completed in two weeks. He wanted to stay until he had at least one baptism, or if not a baptism, at least a convert of his very own. A telegram was delivered asking that someone meet a midnight train on which Elder Whitehead would arrive. Eight young men in bowler hats and heavy topcoats stood conspicuously at the station, wondering which of them might be sent home. As Elder Whitehead got off the train and walked toward the missionaries with a large sealed envelope, Mark was sick with anticipation. Then Elder Lewis opened the letter and learned that he had been recalled to Toronto, where he would serve as mission secretary, and Mark Edward Petersen had been appointed president of the Nova Scotia Conference.

As the presiding officer in Nova Scotia, Mark found that occasionally he was invited to preach before other church groups. On Sunday, January 22, he was called to Tuft's Cove in a howling blizzard to address a small Baptist mission. Mark found a few sectarian hymns that they all knew, and he and his companion, Elder Barnes, spoke to the assembled group. As the elements raged, the elders raised their voices to be heard above the storm. Mark had noticed the two collection plates on the pulpit but had received no instruction for their use. When he stood to announce the closing song, the deacon of the church came running up and explained in horror that Mark had forgotten the collection. Meekly, Mark sat down while the deacon collected seventy-eight cents in pennies and two five-cent pieces.

Mark discovered that among his duties as president of the Nova Scotia Conference was not only pronouncing blessings on the sick but sitting up with them as well. The daughter of a member family named Fredericks had taken seriously ill. Mark, who liked his sleep all his life, stayed with the little girl for three nights while her parents rested. Also as president he traveled to visit the other elders, speaking before groups in rented halls.

Sister Forrest, a Halifax member, provided Mark with his first experience of healing. She had suffered from a bleeding problem for many years and felt that healing by the laying on of hands provided her only hope. Mark and Elder Peacock fasted and prayed for her recovery all day Sunday. In the evening they went to the Forrest home and administered to her. Mark, sealing the anointing, blessed her with certain blessings for which she had secretly prayed for a number of years as well as promised that her recovery would be complete. Months later, when he had returned home, he was pleased to learn in a letter from Sister Forrest that the doctors had pronounced her completely cured.

One Sunday Mark returned to Windsor for a Sunday hall meeting followed by a cottage meeting. He had felt blessed, since becoming the president of the conference, to have received many gifts of the Spirit. On this weekend he enjoyed great inspiration as he spoke. Words and ideas came to him in such abundance that he was sure he truly understood the meaning of an outpouring of the Spirit. As he prepared to return to Halifax, Sister Shaw took him aside and told of a remarkable experience. She said, "As you stood preaching at the hall meeting and also at the cottage meeting, a ball of fire of beautiful color and great brightness stood above your head. Rays of light from the ball were directed upon me. The light continued until you stopped speaking. Then it disappeared."

Sister Shaw said she was wide awake, every faculty alert, and there was no dream or imagination about it. Mark wrote, "How thankful we feel that the fire of the Holy Ghost was actually present with us, and that this manifestation was given to Sister Shaw to strengthen her testimony."

On May 6 Elder Peacock was transferred to the New

Brunswick Conference with headquarters at Moncton. This time it was not an April Fool's joke. He had been Mark's companion since his arrival in the mission field and was a great support in bearing the responsibilities for the conference. On May 12, when all of the missionaries met with President Jensen, the New Glasgow elders reported their first two baptisms in Stellarton. Mark was also told to look for his release in June, when he would have been in the field thirty months.

The next day at the post office, Mark met two women who had briefly investigated the Church at meetings at the McLean home. They passed on the news that Mr. McLean, who had moved his family to Prince Edward Island, was saddened by the passing of his wife two months previously. One of the women had met Captain John McDonald, who was in Halifax for a few days, and had spoken briefly to him. Mark wrote to Emma Marr McDonald with this news of her father.

On June 15 Mark was honorably released from his mission. Two days later he caught a train to Yarmouth, where he boarded a ship for Boston. He arrived after a seventeen-hour ocean trip of 275 miles. For two days he visited Revolutionary War sites, then returned to the ship to continue on to New York. He felt a great surge of patriotism on seeing the Statue of Liberty after living in Canada two and a half years.

In New York he stayed with the elders and visited the Bronx Zoo, the Museum of Natural History, the Woolworth Building, and a New York Giants baseball game. Then he sailed up the Hudson River past Grant's Tomb, the Palisades, West Point, and the Catskills. In Albany he caught a train for Butte, Montana, to visit his twin sister and her family. Following a brief overnight visit, he boarded a train for Salt Lake City.

His missionary journal concludes, "Somehow word of my coming had not reached my family, and I made my way home after thirty months to find the folks all in bed. Now a royal welcome is being accorded me by my friends and relatives here. I am no more an active missionary and am attempting to settle down again to the routine of home life among the Saints."

6

Emma Marr

"Their hearts . . . being knit together in love"
(Colossians 2:2)

Upon his return from Nova Scotia, Mark enrolled at the University of Utah, working for his father after school and on Saturdays. Christian Petersen had hoped his son would become an engineer, thus allowing the family contracting business to expand. But Mark was fascinated by words; he loved to write. One of the great pleasures of his mission resulted from the letters he composed requesting permission to tract and hold street meetings. Newspaper editors, friendly and not, had allowed him to contribute articles on Mormon doctrine to their weeklies. This first transfusion of printer's ink into his bloodstream proved addicting. Throughout the remainder of his eighty-three years, Mark found enormous satisfaction in influencing public sentiment anonymously. For reasons known only to himself, the thrill was in the story, not the byline. If another writer needed credit for an article or even a book, so be it. He rewrote and refined the unpublishable, often giving fledgling authors the boost they needed to continue their work.

During Mark's mission, Emma Marr and Sarah McDonald had written regularly, sending names and addresses of friends and relatives in Nova Scotia, some of whom he visited several times. But the McDonalds were merely members of his home ward. The thought of anything more than a friendship with Emma Marr never entered his head.

Thrilled with his newly discovered journalistic talents, Mark returned to Salt Lake City appreciating vocabulary, literature, and even the grammar of which Emma was so fond.

He liked to listen to her talk and was fascinated by her tales of sailing ships and England. With her, he could share his feelings about Nova Scotia, her birthplace.

While Sarah McDonald enthusiastically welcomed Mark's preaching to her family in Nova Scotia, her feelings were quite different in regard to his courtship of her only daughter. Jack, Emma's older brother, had graduated from engineering school and found a fine position with General Electric. Sarah, herself well educated, had taught school before her marriage. Although estranged from the family, the father, Captain John, had risen to the top of his chosen field. Now Mark Petersen, a part-time student and Saturday carpenter, with no education, no career, and no real job, had become a checker of railroad cars for the Salt Lake Route, which later became part of the Union Pacific. In Sarah's eyes, this made Mark even less desirable as a son-in-law.

Appalled at his lack of education and absence of future promise, Sarah and Jack McDonald did all in their power to discourage the romance. Previously Mark had been welcomed into the bosom of the McDonald home; now he was invited to wait on the porch when he called for Emma Marr. The McDonalds waged a battle against the tall, dark, and handsome suitor, repeatedly pointing out that Emma "will grow tired of wearing cotton stockings." Silk hose would be far beyond the budget of this ill-prepared young man. But Mark persisted, and the courtship progressed quickly. On August 30, 1922, less than eight weeks after he returned home, they became engaged. They were married exactly one year later in the Salt Lake Temple.

Mark wrote, "It was a beautiful day, from the weather point of view, as we went into the temple. When we came out, a cloudburst was in progress. I have never before or since seen such an electric storm and downpour in my life as occurred on our wedding day. We were drenched just coming into the house from the car. But rain or shine, we had our wedding breakfast at my mother's place and were happy." The couple left later that afternoon in Jack McDonald's car

Mark and Emma Marr, in photos taken shortly before their marriage

for a three-day honeymoon in a borrowed cabin at Mount Air, a private canyon just east of Salt Lake City.

This inauspicious beginning launched a strong relationship that would allow each partner to grow as an individual. Much as Mark loved his new wife's thick auburn hair, her diminutive five-foot frame, the unforgettable McDonald blue eyes, and the ready wit, he was most attracted by her brilliant mind. With only a finishing-school education, Emma Marr had managed to learn something about almost everything. She was alert, alive, and alluring. Her knowledge of and feel for the king's English made Mark's new wife his chief supporter but also his most exacting critic. Later she explained to her daughters that their father "was a self-made man— made by myself."

The newlyweds had an apartment in the Bodell Apartments at 55 North Main Street in Salt Lake City. Emma Marr continued to work for a time as a bookkeeper at the Salt Lake Knitting Works. She was horrified and dismayed to discover that during her honeymoon, her mother had dyed her wedding dress black, ostensibly so it could be worn to work.

Emma always suspected that the real motivation was her mother's disapproval of the marriage.

In December 1923, Emma Marr had to undergo a major operation for a tumor in her abdomen. "She was a very sick girl for quite a while," Mark wrote. "She was in the hospital Christmas day, and I had to leave her to go to Lynndyl, Utah, where I worked for the railroad."

Following her illness, Emma Marr realized with delight that she was pregnant. But for some unexplained reason, her physician allowed the pregnancy to go on for almost eleven months. Finally he decided to induce labor and, understand-ing the danger of the situation, invited Mark to witness the birth. Never would the future apostle speak of that day with-out tears welling in his eyes and his voice breaking. As he watched in horror and revulsion, his little son was born dead, literally destroyed by the inept doctor. And Emma Marr's tiny body would never be the same. She bore the scars of a mishandled delivery the rest of her life.

Because of their poverty, the heartbroken young couple could not afford to buy a burial plot for their dead baby. Haunted by their wish for a decent burial, they tried unsuc-cessfully to borrow the money they so desperately needed. Finally Mark's parents offered a place in the Petersen family space in the Salt Lake City Cemetery, and baby boy Petersen

Mark with his sisters, Phoebe and Mona, and his parents, Christian and Christine Petersen

was buried next to where his grandparents, Christian and Christine Petersen, would later be buried.

With spring, Mark's search for local employment was rewarded with a job in the north yards of the Oregon Shortline Railroad. He was hired as a fuel clerk in charge of the records of coal and oil burned by all locomotives on that line. He went to school nights in pursuit of his degree. Emma continued to work as a bookkeeper at Salt Lake Knitting Works.

"During this time I had been trying to obtain work at the *Deseret News,* where I had been employed for a while prior to our marriage, under Horace Walker (father of Robert Walker, the Ogden movie star), who was city editor," Mark wrote. "I called every day from the north yards office asking about a possible vacancy. My calls were so persistent that probably and most likely just to get rid of them, they finally put me to work. But they only paid me $120 a month. I was to be the Church reporter. For this I am now very glad, for it gave me an opportunity to become acquainted with the leading men of the Church."

In the fall of 1925, the Petersens discovered happily that Emma Marr was once more with child. Dr. William T. Ward, a dedicated and skillful physician, undertook the prenatal care, and on July 5, 1926, a baby daughter was safely delivered. As July 4, 1926, fell on a Sunday, Independence Day was celebrated on the day of her birth. The new member of the Petersen family, whom they named Marian, arrived at 4:27 A.M., and by 7 A.M. the ecstatic father was back at work.

The other employees in the editorial department were on hand with congratulations. One of them, future prize-winning author Merlo Pusey, wrote an article about a certain reporter so unusually patriotic that he had arranged to have his child born on Independence Day. This article appeared on the local page of the *Deseret News* under the headline "Are Reporters Loyal? Yes, Daughter Born July 4":

"Many times has Mark E. Petersen of the editorial staff of the Deseret News been called upon to write up the birth of American Independence on the Fourth of July, but Monday he was called on to write about the birth of his first child on Independence Day. The new mother and daughter are doing well at Holy Cross Hospital where Mr. Petersen claimed full responsibility for the patriotic birth."

Eight days later, Marian and her mother came home from the hospital. Emma Marr had been nervous about going to Holy Cross, a Catholic hospital, for the delivery, but the experience proved in all ways a happy one. In Marian's book of remembrance she recorded: "A week after her advent into this veil of tears, Marian was brought home from the hospital to 303 East Sixth South, an apartment building with six apartments. We were in the middle section on the ground floor. In the basement apartment immediately below ours lived the family of Jacob Maag, the janitor. Mrs. Maag was very good to our little family and took care of Marian whenever her parents went out. When Marian was a month old she was christened in the Eighth Ward chapel on the corner of Fifth South and Third East. Mark blessed and named her. What he said is not on record, but it was short. He was very nervous, for he had never before blessed one of his own children."

The new baby filled her parents with delight. Pretty, with dark hair and long eyelashes, she seemed almost like a flower, so Mark tenderly called her Pansy. As with most newborns, Marian didn't always sleep at night. Her father started work at 6 A.M., when often mother and daughter had finally drifted into a sound sleep. A typical note follows:

5:30 a.m.

Marr dear—

Pansy is still sleeping. I hope you have a good sleep. Will you call me at work sometime between 8:30 and 9?

I love you so very dearly—all the time—lots more today than ever before. I said good things for you and Pansy.

Allatime,

Marcus

Emma recorded important events in the baby's life. For example, "About the time Marian was a year old, she was presented by her adoring parents with a kiddie car on which, though unable to walk, she traveled around pretty well. One day she rode out to the back porch and, not stopping in time, continued down the stairs right into the basement. There was plenty of excitement for a while and I was quite frightened, but she wasn't hurt to speak of and the incident was quickly forgotten. About this time Marian caught whooping cough, as did Mark. We could never be sure if she gave it to him or he gave it to her. Anyway, they both had it, and Mark would come home after the quarantine was over and complain how the disease held on—how he had whooped amid the crowds in the Hotel Utah lobby while covering a story."

After the incident on the kiddie car, the family was happy to move to a little court at 661 Green Street. Marian learned to walk at thirteen months and became acquainted with a neighbor's large dog, named Rex, who guarded her. The following February they again moved, this time to 829 East Seventh South.

In May 1929 Mark and Emma bought their first automobile, a Model A Ford. In June they drove to Bryce Canyon, where, to their surprise, they discovered snow and cold. They had planned to sleep in a tent, but, fearful of the low temperatures, they decided to leave three-year-old Marian on the back seat of the new car. There she spent a delightfully warm night, while outside her father and mother nearly froze.

Mark was appointed music critic of the *Deseret News*, a position his wife was eminently qualified to fill. He relied heavily on her judgment as he reviewed films, concerts, and other entertainment. One evening he went to a church on Second South and Second East to cover a concert by a new male singer named Nelson Eddy. The musician's consumption of alcohol was apparent, and when he sang "Mammy's Little Baby Loves Shortnin' Bread," the music critic of the *Deseret News* was convinced that Nelson Eddy loved more than bread.

With the depression in full swing, Mark and Emma felt fortunate to have free tickets to most concerts, and movie

passes as well. Sometimes they were the only patrons in a
theater, for few people could afford the price of admission.
Marian's arrival had put a stop to Emma's working days, so
the press passes provided the couple's main entertainment.
Another never-to-be-forgotten pleasure was to walk the few
blocks from home to Fourth South and Seventh East to "smell
the bread." A bakery at this location opened its windows in the
summertime, permeating the air with the delicious aroma of
freshly made loaves.

After two and a half years as a reporter, Mark was transferred to the copy desk, where he edited the news and wrote
headlines. He had been on that desk about a year when
Horace Walker resigned and John Q. Cannon became city
editor. A short time later the managing editor, Harold Goff,
became ill and died, and Mr. Cannon became managing
editor. Another man had aspired to the position, and when
he was passed over, he resigned. Mark got his job as news
editor. Since Mr. Cannon's time was largely taken up with
writing editorials, he gave little attention to the rest of the
editorial department. Thus the responsibility fell to Mark.

Mr. Cannon died in January 1931, and in February,
another non-newspaperman became the managing editor.
Mark continued in his position as news editor with the
supervision of the news department, but his relations with
the new managing editor were not entirely happy. Mark recalled: "I don't know what was in his mind, but I think it was
a case of being totally unfamiliar with newspaper work and
yet being required at least to pose as the actual manager of
the department. I think he thought I knew more about the
technical operation of the paper than he did. It led to some
misunderstandings, which spread an unhappy feeling. I
never had any ambitions to take any power from him, but I
did try conscientiously to do a good job for the paper regardless of credit or glory."

Life at the *Deseret News* became so difficult for Mark at
this time that he sought out Nicholas G. Smith, a future Assistant to the Twelve who was then Acting Patriarch of the

Church. In a previous patriarchal blessing under the hands of Joseph Keddington, Mark had been promised that he would fulfill a mighty mission at home and abroad and that the time would come that he would be called and set apart as an ambassador of the Lord Jesus Christ. Now he sought another blessing so that he might understand his future and the direction to be taken. Elder Smith told him, in part:

"You have been guarded and protected and led along life's pathway, preserved from evil. The Lord loves you for your desire to play your part nobly before Him. He has given you opportunities to express yourself and to exert influence on others. Be humble, Mark, at all times and prayerful, for Satan has his eye upon you and will shorten your work if possible through causing you to err. Therefore, be prayerful and humble, for Satan cannot molest the humble and pure in heart.

"I bless you that you may measure up to your responsibilities. I bless you that you shall never want for the necessities of life; I bless you that your mind may be clear, that your pen may reach the hearts of thousands of people and they shall feel the influence that comes from you through reading of that which you present unto them. Great responsibilities are coming to you in the community and in the Church. Falter not at any duty; carry on with all your might and you shall be helped. You shall meet difficulties and be able to overcome them as you are faithful. I bless you to live to a goodly age, wielding an influence that shall affect the hearts and minds of those who shall live after you."

Emma also received a blessing, in which she was told, "Marr, the Lord loves you for your devotion to right and righteousness, for the purity of your life, for your willingness to sacrifice to make others happy. Your name shall go down through the generations carried on by the lives of your children and your children's children."

Interpreting his blessing as a message to continue, Mark stayed at the *Deseret News*—and developed ulcers. The general manager at the time also found his relationship with the managing editor uncomfortable and unsatisfactory. Meanwhile, the managing editor's distaste for his young news editor became unbearable, and he gave Mark the sack. As soon as the general manager heard that Mark had been fired, he immediately rehired him, still as news editor. Mark could never really be sure that he was reinstated because of the worth of his work or because of his bosses' dislike for each other. The firings and hirings became quite regular. One fired; the other rehired. Mark's ulcers grew worse, but he survived on rice pudding and Emma's sympathy. Marian's quick smile and bright eyes also helped make life endurable.

Mark continued his writing career. At the time of the Church's centennial in 1930, he was appointed a member of a publicity committee to send news stories and photos to newspapers and magazines throughout North America and Europe. This kept him very busy, and his releases were read by millions of people, so great was the circulation of these publications. Articles he had written appeared in many trade magazines and newspapers in the United States, and some in foreign papers, one being translated into German, his high-school second language. The committee made a great scrapbook from the clippings they received, had it bound, and presented it to President Heber J. Grant, who publicly acknowledged the gift at a subsequent general conference. On October 2, 1930, he sent Mark a fine letter of appreciation signed by himself and his two counselors, Anthony W. Ivins and Charles W. Nibley.

7

New Opportunities

"Stand forth in the work wherewith I have called you"
(D&C 9:14)

In April 1931, the Petersens decided to stop paying rent and buy a house. They had chosen a home outside the Liberty Stake when a new circumstance arose. The very day before they were to sign the mortgage, President Bryant S. Hinckley of the Liberty Stake called Mark to become a member of the high council. At the stake conference on Sunday, April 19, 1931, George Albert Smith, Jr., and Mark were sustained as alternate high councilors. They were ordained high priests and set apart by Elder George F. Richards of the Council of the Twelve in his office in the Salt Lake Temple, where he was president at the time.

"This call put an end to our thoughts of buying a home outside the stake," Mark noted in his journal. "As Emma Marr was expecting another child, we thereupon purchased my father and mother's home at 848 East Sixth South, where we continued to reside until 1941."

Mark's enthusiasm for the newspaper business occasionally led him to cross-purposes with his wife. He carried a press camera in his car, and to Emma it seemed that scooping the "people down the street" was the most important goal in his life. When on the night of August 24, 1931, Emma woke with heavy labor pains, Mark decided that he should hurry to the hospital without dressing or arranging for a baby-sitter for Marian. Then with Emma safely in the hands of Dr. Ward and the good sisters of the Holy Cross Hospital, he could return home, dress, deliver Marian to her grandmother, and go back to the hospital. Emma Marr, certain that her baby might arrive momentarily, agreed to a pajama-clad escort.

As the Petersens raced to the hospital, Mark noticed that the sky was a bright orange. It must be a fire! Sirens shrilled in the night and smoke burned eyes and throats. With five-year-old Marian asleep on the back seat of the car, and Emma up front certain that she was about to deliver, Mark chased the fire engines. Hoping that the opposition newspaper was safely tucked in bed, he wanted a picture of the fire more than anything else. He parked his car as close to the blaze as he could, told Emma he would be right back, and, camera in hand, climbed the nearest telephone pole. He took his pictures, interviewed the firemen, and returned to the car. He also temporarily made an enemy of his wife, who was sure she would give birth to her child by the side of the road like the pioneers. Mark rushed her to the hospital, rushed his film to the *Deseret News* and wrote the story, rushed his daughter to her grandmother's, rushed home and dressed, rushed back to the hospital, and arrived in time to greet his daughter Peggy on August 25, 1931.

Named after her older sister's favorite doll, the new baby was healthy and happy in spite of her parents' adventure on the way to the hospital. Emma Marr's proper British background prevented her acceptance of a nickname for her second daughter, so Peggy became Margaret Elaine on her birth certificate. All family members then had the letters *MAR* at the first of their names.

After an eight-day hospital stay, Emma and her newborn daughter came home with Mark. Waiting in the mailbox was an urgent summons from Captain John Alexander McDonald, who lay ill in a home for retired seamen in Boston. It was the first time any of the McDonalds had heard from the Captain since he had renounced them when Emma was fifteen. Now, all bitterness forgotten, Captain John wished to see his darling Emma Marr. With an active five-year-old and a newborn baby, not to mention her husband's miniscule salary, Emma was unable to go to Boston. But her

*Emma Marr and
Mark with daughters
Marian and Peggy,
1932*

brother, Jack, had an appointment at the General Electric
plant at Schenectady, New York, and Boston was a short train
ride from there.

In Boston Jack arrived at the Retired Sailors home to discover that his father had been hospitalized the day before.
He hurried to the hospital, where a nurse explained that
Captain John was too sick for visitors. She asked Jack to return the next day. This Jack did, only to find his father surrounded by people attempting to revive him. However, the
old man regained consciousness, recognized Jack, and literally died in his arms. Captain John Alexander McDonald was
buried in Nova Scotia near Framboise. Later Mark and Emma
visited the grave and photographed the small monument.

The Petersens' stake president was Bryant S. Hinckley, father of President Gordon B. Hinckley. Marjorie Pay, the future wife of President Hinckley, became Marian and Peggy's favorite baby tender. Emma's mother, Sarah McDonald, had been Relief Society president in the First Ward for a long time. Mark enjoyed retelling the following: "President Hinckley had a farm out in the country and one day, returning in his truck, he saw a young man whom he recognized walking toward home from Liberty Park. He gave the boy a ride and asked him what ward he lived in, and the boy answered, 'The First Ward.' President Hinckley said, 'Well, who is your bishop there?' And the boy replied, 'I am not sure, but I think it is Sister McDonald.'"

On October 9, 1934, Mark was appointed by the First Presidency as a member of the board of directors of the Genealogical Society of Utah. With genealogical conferences to conduct each weekend, Mark hesitated to leave Emma Marr at home with two young daughters and no car. After a diligent search, he discovered an auto that could be purchased for the sum of twenty-five dollars. He presented his money, cash on the barrelhead, and gingerly slid behind the steering wheel. The car seemed unwilling to start, and once started, unwilling to stop. But Mark drove it home thinking he would test it on the way to work. The next day the starter remained silent; the car refused to move. The following morning and every morning thereafter Mark tried to start the car, and his frustration grew with each unsuccessful attempt. Finally, early Saturday morning, he packed his bag and went to the garage. As he cranked the car, the engine immediately sprang to life. The car drove beautifully all the way to the conference and all the way home. The next Monday, again the car refused to start, as it did Tuesday and Wednesday and Thursday and Friday. On Saturday the engine again hummed to the genealogical conference and back. For this reason Marian and Peggy christened it the Genealogical Car. In the seven years Mark had it, not once did it run unless it was headed for conference.

When the general manager of the *Deseret News* retired in 1936, Elder Samuel O. Bennion of the First Council of Seventy was appointed to the position. He turned out to be one of the finest friends Mark ever had. After serving as president of the Central States Mission for more than twenty years, he had been called home to accept a position in the Seventy. Almost immediately afterward he became the manager of the newspaper, so appointed because the president of the Central States Mission also managed Zion's Printing and Publishing Company in Independence, Missouri. The Brethren believed that because of Brother Bennion's experience with that small plant, he would be able to run the Deseret News plant. No one could have been kinder than Brother Bennion. He showed great confidence in Mark, who took pleasure in making sure that this confidence was never betrayed.

Shortly after Elder Bennion's coming to the *News*, the managing editor was called to preside over the British Mission. For some time no one was appointed to succeed him, and so the responsibility continued on Mark's shoulders. During that period the news desk obtained permission to broadcast for fifteen minutes every day on radio station KSL. Mark took over this news broadcast for about two months and greatly enjoyed it.

Elder Bennion provided many opportunities for Mark's development. Occasionally Elder Bennion received an assignment that he disliked, and so he took it upon himself to see that it was filled capably but by someone else. When he was asked to deliver a series of Sunday night sermons on KSL, he instructed Mark to write the speeches. Elder Bennion would deliver them. Soon after the series ended, Mark was called on the carpet by President J. Reuben Clark, Jr., of the First Presidency. President Clark had a finely tuned ear and was sure that the Sunday sermons were more the style of the youngest member of the Genealogical Committee than his esteemed employer. "Who wrote those talks anyway?" President Clark queried. Mark confessed his authorship, and from that day President Clark kept his eye on the young man. He

The Petersen family in the mid-1930s. Back, left to right: Mona Smith (Mark's twin), Betty Smith, Christian and Christine Petersen, Emma Marr, Mark. Front: Barbara Smith, Marian and Peggy Petersen, Frank Smith

chose Mark Petersen as a protégé, and Mark cherished this great man as teacher and example. More than any other General Authority in the Church hierarchy, President Clark gave Mark the opportunity to meet his destiny. And through careful instruction, he made sure the young man was well prepared.

On January 5, 1936, President Bryant S. Hinckley summoned Mark to his home and called him to serve as second counselor in the Liberty Stake presidency. In December, when President Hinckley was called to serve as president of the Northern States Mission in Chicago, J. Percy Goddard was chosen as head of Liberty Stake. He selected Fred M. Michelson as first counselor and Mark as second counselor. On January 7, 1937, Mark was set apart to this office by President Rudger Clawson of the Council of the Twelve.

Mark's love for the newspaper business grew with the years. He completed extension courses from schools with strong journalism departments—Columbia University, Stanford University, the University of Chicago, and the University of California at Los Angeles. He was appointed managing editor, with a glass cubicle in the Deseret News Building on Richards Street just south of Temple Square. With his increased responsibilities, his feelings of proprietorship led him to demand excellence of his staff and himself. Shirt sleeves rolled up and grease pencil ready, he wanted to produce the best newspaper in Salt Lake City.

With a small increase in salary, Mark felt he could afford a new car. Proudly he purchased a bright red Chevrolet, and he was disappointed when the city fathers vetoed his request for a siren to speed him to the office for extras. He developed a calling network that in an emergency could bring the entire news staff to work in less than thirty minutes. His children, trained to judge occurrences by whether or not they happened on the deadline of the rival *Salt Lake Tribune*, delighted in his stories of current events. It was years before the two Petersen daughters realized that not all fathers worked on Thanksgiving and Christmas. Rather than ask his co-workers to miss these family occasions, he routinely covered both holidays every year.

Emma Marr was friendly with her next-door neighbor. Each woman stayed at home with her small children, and visiting over the fence helped pass the time. Each woman also had a husband who was away a great deal. Mark went to Church conferences and the neighbor's husband went to the local tavern. Emma enjoyed it when the neighbor offered sympathy that Mark would desert her for the Church, not realizing that her own husband's drinking absented him from his family even more.

President J. Reuben Clark, because of his national stature as a diplomat and lawyer, had many friends of great influence. He realized that Mark needed an overview of newspaper work if he were to reach his potential. Mark recalled, "President Clark asked me if I would like to visit some other newspapers in the East and probably work on some for a time. I told him I would like that very much." Following that invitation, Mark spent a month in Cincinnati, where he worked on two newspapers, going from one department to another and mailing back reports on what he found to Samuel O. Bennion at the *News*. He worked also at the *New*

York Sun and in Boston at the *Christian Science Monitor*. This trip was very profitable, allowing him to study every department in the newspapers and write detailed notes about their operation, all of which he began to use after he became the general manager of the the *Deseret News*.

Ever since his mission, Mark had enjoyed speaking in public, and as his travels for the Genealogical Society decreased, he found himself addressing at least one sacrament meeting somewhere every Sunday. And because Emma usually had a musical assignment for sacrament meeting, Mark was elected to tend his daughters. Neither Marian nor Peggy had any fondness for lengthy speeches, and they asked him often if he didn't know any two-and-a-half-minute talks.

Mark was fascinated by the Book of Mormon and the promises to the Lamanites. He often spoke of the great numbers of Lamanites in Mexico, Central America, and South America. According to the studies he had read, there were about nine million Indians in the thirties. On their way home after a speech on the subject, Marian and Peggy registered their complaint at "having to hear about our nine million Lamanites again tonight."

Emma had very good reason to give her daughters to her husband when she performed. As ward organist, she was often called upon to play at funerals, and because the funerals were usually scheduled during the noon hour, no baby tenders were available. During one very lengthy service she was startled to look up and see Marian gently rocking the casket as the speaker droned on. Peggy, also a problem, seemed to be overly sensitive to pitch, and whenever a singer was slightly off key, the younger Petersen daughter covered her ears with her hands and screamed.

In 1940 Mark and Emma purchased a lot at 1457 Westminster Avenue, and Mark's father built their new home. In the summer of 1941 the move was accomplished, but Mark's release from the Liberty Stake presidency was delayed until October while he completed some projects already underway.

Mark, in a photograph taken when he studied newspapers in the East

With failing health due to severe diabetes, Elder Samuel O. Bennion was replaced as manager of the *Deseret News*. Greatly loved by all the staff, especially Mark, he had brought morale to a high level. He adored Marian and Peggy and enjoyed buying them treats. A very happy relationship ended with his retirement.

Brother Bennion's release resulted in Mark's appointment as general manager of the paper on August 1, 1941, just before the United States entered World War II. After the initial announcement of his appointment in the press, Mark let it be known that neither his name nor his face should appear in the *Deseret News*. Any staffer making the mistake of mentioning him in an article would be fired. And after his adventures with his former bosses, Mark was an expert on hirings and firings.

The paper had been running in the red for a number of years. Part of the problem was a practice that the manager be a Church official, not necessarily a newspaperman. Fortunately Mark had worked his way through all the departments and most of the jobs. This fact, combined with the training that President Clark had so fortuitously provided, gave Mark the opportunity to create a money-making metropolitan newspaper. Another plus was his relationship with the publisher, Albert E. Bowen of the Council of the Twelve. Elder Bowen, an astute attorney and wise businessman, listened to Mark's ideas and was willing to try them.

The first thing the two men did was to raise the monthly subscription rate from sixty-five to seventy-five cents. This one innovation brought them into the black almost overnight. They then determined to offer more news to compensate the reader for the added expense. The staff, knowing Mark asked them to do nothing he would not do himself, stood solidly behind him in giving their best effort.

Society was the one department that frustrated Mark. He knew that the city's social leaders could influence attitudes toward the paper. Mark was acquainted with an impeccably dressed, supremely well-mannered society matron who knew all the right people and had an aristocratic British accent. With Brother Bowen's blessing (the woman was a friend of his wife), Mark hired Dorothy Watkiss as society editor. Star of the feature writing was Howard Pearson, as good a newspaperman as any in the area. Dorothy discovered everything about everyone, and Howard wrote it all down. Soon the *Deseret News* society pages became more popular than the funny papers.

With the pressure for better coverage and greater accuracy, considerable tension could be felt among the staff as deadlines approached. Occasionally a real blooper would occur with a misspelled name or word in a headline. Marian and Peggy soon learned to recognize Brother Bowen's voice. When his discerning eye caught an error, he was on the telephone regardless of the hour, and his complaint could be heard by anyone within shouting distance of the phone.

If a staffer at the *News* had a problem, Mark usually was approached and his advice sought and heeded. In return, he regularly asked for ideas and criticism from his staff. He respected their suggestions and they respected his. Even as general manager, he still became very excited about a good story, especially an exclusive. At West Temple and First South, just a block from the Deseret News building, stood a long shantylike building occupied by shops run by the Oriental community. When Mark heard that an opium den there was about to be raided, he thought it might be educational to let his children witness the wages of sin. Arriving home, he could find only his younger daughter. He asked her if she would like to go to a drug raid. Puzzled as to the definition of drugs, she nevertheless knew what a raid was, and off they went.

As the vigor and accuracy of the paper grew, so did its audience, among whom was President Heber J. Grant. As a former newspaper publisher, he was well qualified to evaluate, and some of his evaluations were painful for Mark. President Grant read the paper the moment it hit the streets. Then, if he found an article to which he objected, he would pick up the phone and say, "Mark, get over here." Mark never asked who was calling or where "here" was. He just headed for 47 East South Temple. President Grant, with the paper spread before him on his desk, always circled the offending story, and he emphasized his words by tapping a long forefinger on the circle as he spoke. He could be scathing in his criticism—and often was. But when the bluster had passed, he was immediately remorseful and hoped he had not injured Mark's feelings. He would call to Joseph Anderson, his secretary and right-hand man, "Joseph, can't we find a book for Mark Petersen?" Joseph usually had a book at the ready, and President Grant would inscribe the volume with a flourish of his pen. Smiling wryly, Mark often explained that this was the way he acquired his extensive library.

One Sunday Mark had just returned home from his Church duties when he turned on the radio and heard the shocking news that the Japanese had bombed Pearl Harbor. The United States was at war. At forty-one, he was two years too old for the draft. But many of the staff were the perfect age for military service, and Mark found himself running a paper with any help he could get. Newsprint was scarce, and trips to paper mills in the Northwest became a necessity. Not sure where the next roll of paper was coming from, he vowed he would never again find himself in such a position of need. As soon after the war as Brother Bowen could be persuaded, Mark would insist that the *Deseret News* own its own source of paper.

With only a skeleton staff, Mark found himself more of a newspaperman than ever. An appointment to the Gasoline Ration Board also took time. He learned a great deal about human nature as he listened to individuals explaining why their lives required extra petrol. Correspondence from the *News* staff members serving in the armed forces added a fascinating dimension to the war news, vividly supplementing the teletype reports. Mark thrilled to see the country unite, accepting half-empty grocery shelves, saving fats, and riding the bus. Everyone wanted success on the war front and gracefully endured inconvenience with a smile. Service stars appeared in the windows of homes with relatives in the armed forces. The sight of "Old Glory" brought a lump to the throat. A warm feeling of brotherhood pervaded the country.

On April 10, 1943, Mark was called to the general board of the Sunday School. He was also serving on the high council of the Highland Stake, a fast-growing church unit. Apparently the powers that be noticed the stake's rate of growth, for on May 16, 1943, Elders Joseph Fielding Smith and Harold B. Lee effected a division. The Sugarhouse Stake was born with Mark called to be first counselor in the presidency. Thus, he resigned from the Sunday School general board after less than two months.

Mark's religious development was a constant part of his life all through these years. He loved the scriptures and studied them. He devoured newspapers, newsmagazines, trade journals, astronomy and science texts, biographies, and history, but always the scriptures. Emma Marr had a taste for mysteries, which she read with relish. On occasion she enjoyed the Saturday afternoon horror shows at the Capitol Theater. Mark didn't have time for such frivolities. There was too much to learn. If ever a student was natural born, it was Mark. He gloried in discovery. At home he always had a book in his hand. Neither of his daughters ever thought to complain that there was nothing to do. The Petersens all read and read and read.

Music added enjoyment to their home life, and even before living room furniture, a baby grand piano was purchased for Emma. The family often sang to her expert accompaniment, with Emma, who never forgot a word to a song, whispering the coming verse as she played its introduction. Life seemed to settle into a pleasant routine.

8

Called to the Twelve

"I am ordained a preacher, and an apostle"
(1 Timothy 2:7)

Since he had become managing editor, Mark's troubles at the *Deseret News* had disappeared except in one area—no one had thought to change his salary. He wished—and Emma especially hoped—that someone, anyone, might notice that the general manager's paycheck remained at managing-editor level while the other employees received regular raises.

But Mark's journalistic talents were not unnoticed nationally. When a San Diego newspaper offered him a management position at triple the money, he and Emma seriously considered the options. He knew that he had climbed as high as he could go at the *Deseret News*. The president of the publishing company and the chairman of the board of directors were not only one and the same, but always a General Authority. Mark thought that let him out. A family council, with each of the girls expressing her feelings, resulted in a tentative vote for San Diego.

Then the hectic combination of newspaper and church work, combined with duties in the Kiwanis Club, Utah Manufacturers, Knife and Fork Club, and the Chamber of Commerce, exacted their toll, and Mark developed a cough he could not shake. Finally, near the end of February 1944, he decided to stay in bed for a weekend. Most people rest while ill in bed. Mark rested by reading. He noticed that every time he opened his scriptures, a reference to the duties of apostles or some other mention of the apostleship lay on the page before him. The more he tried to ignore this strange happening, the more it became apparent that he was receiving some sort of a message.

One night he fell into a deep sleep and had a dream. The very existence of the dream made him uncomfortable because he rarely dreamed. The subject of the dream was appalling. He could see the lead headline of the front page of the *Deseret News* with a terrible mistake in it. The headline read "Lyman R. Richard Dies." How could the copy desk make such an error and reverse the order of Elder Richard R. Lyman's name? He was absolutely certain that regardless of the manpower shortage, he would lose his job because of it. President Grant, President Clark, and Brother Bowen would nail him to the wall! He woke with a jolt. "I was responsible for the newspaper, and to think of Elder Lyman's name on the front page all scrambled up made me almost sick, even in the dream," he recalled.

At six o'clock on Monday morning Mark hurried to work, and as soon as the first edition was put to bed, he called Henry Smith, the Church reporter. Had Henry heard of any illness in the Council of the Twelve? How long since he had seen Richard R. Lyman? Why didn't Henry run over to 47 East South Temple just to test the water?

Henry returned with the news that Elder Lyman was fine and in his office. But Mark could not shake the feeling that some terrible accident or swift-moving illness was about to strike down Elder Lyman, and that he himself would replace him in the Twelve. One of Mark's strongest personality traits was his humility. He was totally unimpressed with himself, and he had certainly never promoted himself for a church position. But he knew President Grant would call him to the Twelve. So much for San Diego.

"Then on a very fateful day, Joseph Anderson came over to the office at the *Deseret News* and told me that President Grant wanted the little notice that was in the envelope which he handed me placed on the front page of the newspaper. He spelled out exactly how he wanted it used—that it was to be placed in a two-column box at the upper left-hand corner of the page, and that was all. It was a plain announcement, but no news story was to accompany it. When I read it, to my horror I saw that Brother Lyman had been excommunicated from the Church.

"I followed the directions and put the box on the front page in the upper left-hand corner. The Brethren asked also if I would see to it that the *Tribune* got the notice, but John Fitzpatrick refused to run the story until after we printed it. He couldn't believe his eyes. After we had published it, the *Tribune* ran it the next day. The *Telegram* was missed entirely because Mr. Fitzpatrick was afraid to run it there until he had actually seen it in the *Deseret News*. The *Deseret News* and the *Telegram* were both evening papers published at the same hour, and the next night it was cold news."

Mark began to feel nervous about the second part of his dream in which he took Elder Lyman's place. A few days before April conference he received a telephone call from Joseph Anderson asking him to come to see President Grant—but not the usual "Mark, get over here" at all. At the office, Brother Anderson told him that President Grant had not yet arrived and asked him to sit down. Soon Mark heard the side door near the Lion House open and knew that President Grant was being brought in from his car. The President had had a stroke that paralyzed his left leg. As Mark related, "I can still hear the dragging of that one foot as he came along the marble floor. I knew exactly what he was coming for. When he came in, he shook hands with me. He had been a great friend to me over the years. He had known Emma Marr and her mother in England and was interested in me from that standpoint as well as my being a newspaperman. He sat down and told me that the Brethren had appointed me the new member of the Council of the Twelve. I said, 'President Grant, I have known for some weeks that this was coming.' I told him about my dream. He shook my hand warmly and told me that the Lord had given me the right impression. I was sustained the following Sunday, April 7, 1944, in general

The Council of the Twelve in 1944. Seated, left to right: George Albert Smith, George F. Richards, Joseph Fielding Smith, Stephen L Richards, John A. Widtsoe, Joseph F. Merrill. Back, left to right: Charles A. Callis, Albert E. Bowen, Harold B. Lee, Spencer W. Kimball, Ezra Taft Benson, Mark E. Petersen

conference. I felt so weak and young and so inadequate, as, of course, I was all of those things."

When Mark's call was announced in the *Deseret News* with a headline of his own on the front page, some of the old-timers wondered if they would lose their jobs for breaking his rule against running his picture and his name in the paper. After the evening edition came off the press, another smaller edition was run for the employees. One of the type-setters changed the headline on the front page to read: "LDS Quorum of the Twelve Goes to the Dogs," with a subhead, "They Chose a Great Dane."

Because of his stroke, President Grant was unable to go to the temple, so Mark was set apart in the First Presidency's boardroom at 47 East South Temple on April 20, 1944. President Grant could not stand for any length of time. He sat in his chair, and Mark knelt before him and was ordained the sixty-fourth member of the Council of the Twelve in this dispensation.

As a memento of the occasion, President Grant gave the Petersens a delicate watercolor. On the paper backing of the painting, he wrote his name and the date. So great was Mark's regard for President Grant that he said he would like to hang the painting to the wall and the autograph for all to see.

In his blessing President Grant said: "Remember that humility in the Church of God is strength and power above everything else. Remember that whenever we trust to ourselves, we are walking upon dangerous ground." This statement could be a quotation from Mark's missionary journal. In his first speech as an apostle, Mark declared, "I know that without the help of the Lord I am powerless to do any good in the ministry; but I know that if I live righteously He will be with me," again echoing the lessons learned in Nova Scotia.

From the time that the Petersens moved to Westminster Avenue, they passed a certain house on the corner of Diestel Road and Sunnyside Avenue almost every day. The reason that they noticed the house was Emma's insistence that it should be in England. With ivy growing over its brick walls, it backed on a ravine lined with fruit trees. Emma said it looked like a home she remembered in Liverpool. Soon the girls referred to it as "Mother's house," and if Emma said nothing when they passed, they would repeat her reasons for its charm as they drove by 851 Diestel Road on their way downtown.

One day they noticed that "Mother's house" was for sale. When Mark and Emma investigated, the price was right and the interior marvelously British. Nothing would do but that Emma should have that house. Her bookkeeping abilities carried over to her running of the family budget, and by hook or by crook, she had managed to make double payments on the Westminster Avenue property, so she and Mark had burned the mortgage just a few short months before. With a paid-for home as security, Mark made the rounds of what he considered to be the good lending institutions, those with Church connections, to borrow enough money to tie up the new house while he disposed of the old. But his

*Mark in the doorway
of the Petersen home
on Diestel Road*

loan applications were soundly refused wherever he went. His special affection for First Security Bank developed when he approached the Eccles family, who owned the bank, and their only question was, "How much do you want and how soon do you need it?" On his signature, they gave him the money. Emma had her English home.

The best part of the Diestel Road residence was its location in Bonneville Ward. Soon after they moved in, the ward moved from sharing the old Yale Ward building to a lovely new building on Bonneview Drive. The Bonneville Ward organ, an unusually fine instrument, became a vital part of Emma Marr's life. Given her own key to the chapel, she walked the two short blocks to the church, where she practiced daily. With Mark traveling every weekend, she was free to resume her musical career. She enjoyed playing for the meetings, especially with the choir. Above the organ and behind the choir seats, a lovely stained-glass window depicting Jesus in the Garden of Gethsemane set the stage for the meetings and added a special feeling to sacrament time.

At home Mark used his carpentry skills to finish a large room in the attic, where the family Ping-Pong table drew him and Emma many evenings. Her serve was deadly, and she loved to blow her opponents out of the game. No woman could be more kind to a person in trouble than she, but put a Ping-Pong paddle in her hand and she was merciless.

On Diestel Road with property extending down to the Red Butte stream, Mark was able to indulge his love of gardening and become a beekeeper as well. The Petersen family always owned at least one dog and sometimes several cats. If a fierce, foaming, wild-eyed animal ran full speed at Mark and Emma, it would be to lick their faces, not to bite them. With the family cocker spaniel at his heels, Mark liked to don his bee hat and gloves, old heavy trousers, and a long-sleeved shirt and collect the honey. To say that he looked disreputable would be flattering. With a swollen-nosed, bee-bitten reddish dog happily trotting behind, a ragged man in a heavily veiled hat wandered the gully flapping the loose soles of his shoes as he walked. His daughters, not yet at an age to understand that someone who wore a white shirt, suit, and tie every day might enjoy old clothing occasionally, pretended not to know him if their friends asked who he was. Peggy once told a neighbor that he was the gardener, which, of course, was true.

The previous owners of 851 Diestel Road had added a sun room with a flat roof behind the kitchen. The rest of the house with its cathedral ceilings and high-pitched shingles sent Emma into architectural ecstasies, but the flat roof attracted Mark. For the first time in his life he had a place for his telescope, which he had purchased so many years ago. When the landlady's son had come bursting into his mission lodgings to tell him to rush outside to see the northern lights, no one knew that the sight might prove addicting and that Mark would become an astronomy enthusiast for the rest of his life. The influence of President David O. McKay, who loved to think of all the life on other planets and often spoke with Mark about the immensity of space, solidified his interest in the stars. He began subscribing to astronomy magazines and reading all the books he could find on the solar system and beyond.

Emma's mother, Sarah McDonald, had always insisted on living alone in the First Ward. Mark had paid her rent and given her spending money, and she was happy to be independent in the Scottish tradition. She had served as Relief Society president into her seventies. One day, while on a Relief Society assignment at Welfare Square, she tripped and fell over a box. In excruciating pain, she realized immediately that her hip was broken. Because the people in the immediate vicinity thought that seventy-year-olds didn't know much, they insisted on pulling her to her feet and making her walk to the car. Finally it became apparent that she was badly hurt, and she was rushed to the hospital, where her hip was pinned. Now in her late eighties, she still experienced difficulty in walking. Thus, she objected hardly at all when Mark and Emma insisted that she come to live with them. The new house had an apartment in the basement that was rented to students, so Emma was never alone while Mark traveled. And if both the Petersens were away, the students could look after Sarah. Jack, her son, also lived nearby. So the move was made, and Sarah was given the master bedroom overlooking the front porch, where she could watch the neighborhood comings and goings and enjoy the sunshine and garden.

If she had not outlived all her friends, leaving the First Ward might have seemed difficult to Sarah. However, from the time she first entered Bonneville Ward chapel, she realized that she had found home. Regardless of the expertise of the Gospel Doctrine leader, Sarah always found something to add or correct in the lesson. As the teacher built toward a dramatic climax, Sarah unhesitatingly made comments that broke up the class. On Fast Day, she seldom missed bearing her testimony at great length. She ruled the Relief Society. She ruled the ward. All this could have been terrible had she not sparkled with wit and always spoke with kindness. She had fun and so did everyone else. Sarah discovered that she

*Sarah McDonald,
Emma Marr's
mother*

was very popular with her neighbors, who found in her a good listening ear. The Petersens were kept busy ushering all sorts of persons into her sitting room to bare their souls and partake of her cheerful advice.

When the Petersens' granddaughter Drew was in law school at BYU, she clerked a few months in Senator Jake Garn's office in Washington, D.C. On her last day, she was invited into the Senator's inner office to have her picture taken with him and her training evaluated. As she got up to leave, she mentioned that she was Peggy Petersen's daughter. Senator Garn pulled her back into the office, shut the door, sat her on the couch, and for thirty minutes told "Sarah Mc-Donald stories" of things that, as a priest, he had witnessed from the sacrament table in Bonneville Ward.

At the time Mark and Emma were married, Sarah was less than enthusiastic about her new son-in-law. Whether or not her private opinion of Mark changed, she never revealed; but often, while speaking of him, she would say that although he was an apostle, he definitely had some improvements to make (particularly in his gardening clothing).

Sarah died at age ninety-four in her own bed on Diestel Road, having been lovingly cared for by her family and countless friends. Her funeral in Bonneville Ward was worthy of this loyal daughter of Zion, but it lacked one thing. For the first time, she interrupted none of the participants.

On May 15, 1944, with so many of the youth of the Church still in the armed services, Mark initiated the LDS servicemen's edition of the *Church News*. Under such headings as "Advice from Our Leaders," "Bits from Your Own Letters," "I Want to Know," "Gems from the Prophet's Teachings," "What's Going On," and "Physical Fitness," Mark wrote or edited regular columns in the clear, crisp style so familiar in his *Church News* editorials. From its inception until the last edition on July 15, 1948, he enjoyed putting out this monthly paper all by himself.

With the death of President Grant in 1945, for the first time Mark stood in the circle while a new president of the Church was set apart. (This solemn experience was to be repeated for four other prophets.) President George Albert Smith succeeded President Grant. As the junior member of the Twelve, Mark experienced many moving and impressive events. Among the most striking was President Smith's restoration to health. During the time he had been president of the Council of the Twelve, as well as throughout most of his life, his health was very poor. He traveled to a stake conference each weekend but returned exhausted and weak, and often had to spend the time virtually bedridden until the next Thursday meeting of the Twelve. Then he would conduct the meeting, go to a conference for the weekend, and return to his sickbed. Some of the Twelve wondered how he could possibly carry on the many duties of the presidency. To complicate matters, the centennial of the arrival of the pioneers in Salt Lake Valley approached. Strong leadership would be imperative if the international attention on the event were to produce the desired results. To perform his labors, vigor was required.

From the time of his setting apart, President Smith received a restoration of his health, and he was able to work tirelessly and successfully. To Mark, who had served with him when he seemed a very sick man, President Smith's vitality was an amazing miracle. Whenever friends spoke of healings within the Church, Mark thought of the invalid who became well.

Mark's testimony grew as he saw two presidents of the Church in action. Each responded to the need of his time in such a way that Mark could not doubt their callings. President Grant had all the qualities needed in the Church at the time he was prophet. He had forged ahead to bring the Saints through the depression and see the membership grow to 937,050. President Smith, who was known for his kindness and great love for his fellowmen, taught the Saints to be aware of their neighbors. He reminded them of the Christlike virtures that should dominate their lives.

The first apostle called by President Smith was Elder Matthew Cowley. The doctors had warned Elder Cowley that because of his heart disease, living at the high altitude of Salt Lake City could be fatal. But Elder Cowley cared only for the work of the Lord and believed that his life was little enough to give for the gospel. As he and Mark sat together at meetings, a close friendship developed.

President J. Reuben Clark was opposed to flying. He felt that airplanes were dangerous and unhealthy. Once President Clark, Mark Petersen, and Matthew Cowley journeyed by train to Washington, D.C., where they made J. Willard Marriott the stake president. General conference was to be held the next weekend. President Clark and his companions spent four days returning to Salt Lake City by train, only to discover that the new stake president had left Washington by plane the morning they were to arrive home and had still beaten them. The two newest apostles decided on the spot that they would take to the air.

At this time, the four youngest members of the quorum were Spencer W. Kimball, Ezra Taft Benson, Mark E. Petersen, and Matthew Cowley. When a General Authorities' dinner was planned, these four offered to sing a quartet as part of the entertainment. Harold B. Lee accompanied them on the piano. Because they dealt with ponderous matters most of the time, they decided to add some humor to the occasion, selecting a song called "Herpicide," which told of the remarkable powers of a hair restorer by that name. Elders LeGrand Richards and Milton R. Hunter were led to chairs on the stage and draped in white sheets as if for a haircut. Mark and company sang with gusto about Herpicide's being "the greatest thing on earth to make the hair grow—makes a head of hair just like a scarecrow." They surrounded the two men and pretended to rub the Herpicide into their bald scalps as they sang. But when the quartet stepped back to display the results of the hair restorer, Elder Richards was sporting a red wig and Elder Hunter a barrister's. All four sang well and their song was technically perfect. As public speakers or singers, their enunciation left nothing to be desired. The real problem was the low origin of the song. After the program, only one person came forward to comment. Levi Edgar Young, always the gentleman, felt that something should be said. His remark left quartet and accompanist aching with laughter: "Gentlemen, the *words* were beautiful."

Elders Kimball and Petersen received many assignments together. The Church had not yet grown to the point that a stake division called for only one member of the Twelve. These two men, although low in seniority, were high in insight into human beings. Interviews that they conducted for stake callings were unusually perceptive, and many Saints found themselves telling the two apostles of feelings never before revealed to another person. So successful was the team that the stakes they set up thrived and became leaders in Church activity. Many of the Twelve ahead of them in seniority were afflicted by health problems, so stake divisions became almost a weekly occurrence for Elders Kimball and Petersen. One of the older Brethren, whose longevity had left poor physical health but an intact sense of humor, christened them "the butchers" because they cut up so many stakes.

On one occasion in the Northwest, as they struggled with interviews long into the night, they knelt in prayer at midnight and both independently received the impression that a certain man should be the new president. Rather than wake the family, they waited until the Sunday morning of stake conference to call on him at his home. His wife was serving breakfast as they entered the room, and the soon-to-be president sat surrounded by his children. Elder Kimball said, "We have come to call you as president of the stake." The man replied, "I knew you were coming. Last night my eight-year-old dreamed of my call and saw you in her dream. When she described two apostles, one short, one tall, I knew it was true."

When four enormous stakes in the Salt Lake Valley were to be made into six, the two apostles were assigned to do the "butchering." With detailed maps, including stake boundaries, streets, and streams, they puzzled as to how to make the changes with as little pain as possible for the stake members. Finally, after almost half a year, the two moved ahead.

The decision to choose one particular stake president came late on a Saturday night. Mark loved his sleep and had on occasion horrified Emma by walking through the living room loudly winding his alarm clock when party guests stayed overlong. His work at the *News* demanded early rising, so he respected the need for sleep in others as well. Thus, when Elder Kimball announced at 11:30 P.M. that they were going to make a call on the president-to-be, Mark objected loudly. They compromised by agreeing to drive past the house. If the lights were on, they would go in. If the lights were off, they would return the next morning. When they stopped outside the home, they saw all the lights shining brightly. Mark thought they might be interrupting a party, but Elder Kimball said, "Let's go!"

As the two young apostles rang the bell, the wife opened the door and told them her husband was expecting them. The man explained that a few days before, he had been given the impression that he would be called as stake president and that the call would come on Saturday night, so he had turned on all the lights and waited.

Once when Elder Kimball was out of the country, Mark took Elder Eldred G. Smith, the Patriarch to the Church, with him to divide a stake. All day they interviewed possible candidates in the stake, but Mark felt that he had not met his man. Finally, after five very discouraging hours, he asked the stake president if there might not be some other priesthood holder worthy to be interviewed. The president said, "The only man I haven't sent in is the man who should be the next president of the stake, but he is too ill to serve. It would kill him."

Mark and Elder Smith prayed for guidance, then summoned the man. At the interview he explained that his doctor suggested he work only part time and participate in no other activities that might tire him. Mark called a physician friend, described the man's health problems, and asked if he could be made stake president. The doctor said it would kill him. Mark prayed and again received the same impression: this man should be called as president of the stake. So he telephoned the man's own medical adviser, and this doctor also insisted that a stake call would positively prove fatal.

After more interviews and more prayers, Mark wrote three names on a piece of paper—the names of two men who would do but inspiration said no, and the name of the man with the illness. He then asked Elder Smith to kneel with him and seek guidance in choosing the new head of the stake. When they rose from their prayer, only one name remained on the paper—the name of the sick brother.

Mark hesitantly asked the stake president to bring the man in for an interview. When he arrived, Mark told him of the paper with the three names that changed after prayer to his name only. The man said, "Then you had better heal me."

After administering to the man who was too sick to serve, Mark and Elder Smith set him apart as stake president. He labored in good health for ten years, in better health than ever before in his life.

When Mark was called to Australia to create a new stake, he had difficulty finding a priesthood holder with enough Church experience to fill the position. For hours he had interviewed all the Melchizedek Priesthood holders in the area. He was delighted with the spirit of the men and could sense their testimony and strength, but he needed someone with more experience. Finally he asked the mission president if there might not be just one other person whom he had not interviewed. The president replied that one such man had just moved into the area. Since he really did not know much about him, he had not contacted him to be interviewed. Mark sent for the newcomer.

Who should walk into the room but a former counselor from a stake in Great Britain! Mark himself had set him apart. Now they had their stake president. The man then told Mark, "After the shipbuilding industry foundered in our town back home, my wife and I decided to move to Canada. I drew the money out of the bank, sold my house, packed my goods, and bought the tickets. Then I dreamed a dream that was so real that I woke my wife in the middle of the night. I told her that we were moving to Australia. She asked why Australia and not Canada. I replied that the Lord wanted us to go to Australia but I couldn't tell her why. We moved to Australia, where we found excellent work in the shipyards, but I haven't known until now why the Lord wanted us here." With such faith, how could a better man be found for the job?

As they traveled together, Elders Kimball and Petersen discovered they had many things in common. But one characteristic they did *not* share was their need for rest. Elder Kimball, impatient with wasting time sleeping, often rose at four o'clock to begin his work. Mark, on the other hand, moved at a frantic pace, then collapsed and slept hard for

*Christine and Christian Petersen surrounded by their descendants
in a photo taken around 1948*

eight hours. When they roomed together, Mark loved the association and the conversation, but he dreaded the light
going on at four in the morning.

The two men enjoyed swimming and found it the most
practical way to get their exercise. When they walked, they
were stopped every few feet to shake hands or greet someone. But no one waved at them down in the deep end of the
pool. Their heavy schedule left little time for aquatics until
they hit upon a wonderful idea. They invented an uncle,
Uncle Gym by name, and gave him a daily appointment. With
the old Deseret Gym almost outside their offices, Uncle Gym
demanded only forty-five minutes. After seeing him, they
continued their work, relaxed and happy.

9

Editor and Writer

"Write the things which thou hast seen"
(Revelation 1:19)

Responsibilities at the *Deseret News* prevented Mark's taking lengthy trips for the Church. Working two full-time jobs required that he resign from the board of directors of the Salt Lake Chamber of Commerce, but since the Bonneville Knife and Fork Club met at night, he was able to enjoy a year as president in 1945. The Salt Lake Kiwanis Club had provided him with the means to lunch with many of his friends, but unfortunately, Kiwanis met on the same day as did the Council of the Twelve. Mark had always claimed that he was too young for the Rotary Club, which met on another day, but he missed the association with the business community, so he decided to join that group. When the Kiwanians heard that their former vice-president was considering becoming a Rotarian, they immediately made him an honorary life member of Kiwanis. So ended his plans for Rotary. Mark never forgot that at his last Kiwanis meeting, the members, to show respect for his call, neither smoked nor drank tea or coffee.

By 1950 it had become apparent that Mark could not do justice to both the newspaper and his Church calling without breaking his health. Of course, his first consideration was the performance of his duties as a special witness. He was therefore released as general manager and was named president of the Deseret News Publishing Company and chairman of the board of directors. He also became a member of the executive board of the Great Salt Lake Council of the Boy Scouts of America. His release as general manager of the *News* made

Mark at typewriter

him even more determined that the paper continue to be strong, backed by a paper mill. A newspaper war of sorts erupted in Salt Lake City with the *Tribune* and the *News* competing for readers. As the *News* grew in strength, the *Salt Lake Telegram*, also an evening paper, had difficulties. Mark received permission from the First Presidency to purchase the struggling paper from the Kearns family, but John Fitzpatrick declined the offer. Mark persisted, however, and when the *Deseret News* finally acquired the *Telegram*, he framed the last issue of the *Telegram* and the first issue of the combined *Deseret News and Salt Lake Telegram* and hung them side by side in his office like the head of a prize moose. The paper later dropped the last four words in the title and once again became known as the *Deseret News*.

When David O. McKay became president of the Church

in 1951, he wanted the *Deseret News* to continue as a strong voice of the Church. Believing that the *News* had grown as large as it could without a Sunday edition, President McKay gave orders for seven-day publication. Mark traveled to all the areas of the *News* circulation and called meetings to explain to the Saints the necessity for a seven-day paper in this particular period. To avoid possible opposition, he prepared his audiences for the message from President McKay by beginning each meeting with the hymn "We Thank Thee, O God, for a Prophet." The opposition never materialized.

As president and chairman of the board of the Deseret News Publishing Company, Mark felt full responsibility for the future of the paper. He reasoned that there was no way the *Tribune* and the *Deseret News* could continue to give excellent and total news coverage if staff and production costs continued to escalate. Because of dramatic new mechanical developments, the presses then in use needed to be replaced. Linotype operators, the former backbone of the printing industry, were on their way to obsolescence.

Mark approached Elder Albert E. Bowen with a startling idea. Why continue this newspaper war? Why not unite with "the people down the street"? Why have duplicate equipment costing millions of dollars and each used only half the time? The *Tribune* press runs would conflict in no way with the publication of the *News*. Why not buy one press for two newspapers?

Recovering from his initial shock, Elder Bowen felt that this request needed First Presidency approval. Mark asked for an appointment with President Clark. As J. Reuben Clark grew older, his phenomenal mental capabilities never diminished. Immediately he understood Mark's proposal and examined it with a businessman's expertise, a lawyer's shrewdness. The lawyer spoke first. "It's against the law."

Mark had heard that Congress, realizing that printing costs were forcing some newspapers out of business, had considered legislation enabling two competing newspapers to use the same printing plant without violating the Sherman

Antitrust Act. President Clark listened thoughtfully, then made a decision. Mark could go to Texas to observe the two newspapers now planning a similar operation and bring back as many details of the contracts and organization as possible. With all available data compiled, the First Presidency could reach a conclusion. Mark had sailed over the first hurdle. As he explained to Emma Marr President Clark's response to his proposal, "He said it was illegal, but he didn't say no."

In his years of newspaper management, Mark had done his work at his office. But when he arrived in Texas, he discovered that the key man from whom he must extract the most vital information liked to conduct business in a cocktail lounge, the darker the better. He also liked to talk at great length on any subject on which he was knowledgeable and a few on which he wasn't. After the second day of pub crawling, having made no headway at all, Mark was ready to throw up his hands and forget the whole idea. Finally his host began describing the setup between his paper and the opposition. For two hours he detailed organization and contracts while Mark scribbled notes on a menu. As he concluded, the Texan drawled, "But why should I tell you this when I did all the work?"

Mark returned to Salt Lake City with the information and vowing never to drink another ginger ale. His three-day liquid diet paid off as he presented his proposal to the First Presidency. Their tentative approval resulted in Mark's approaching John Fitzpatrick, the *Tribune* publisher. Mr. Fitzpatrick was very aware that the newspaper competition in Salt Lake City had driven costs to unbearable heights. Both papers refused to back off even to save money, a no-win situation for everyone. Realizing that the staffs might start speculating if either man visited the other's office, the two set a meeting on the neutral ground of the Hotel Utah Coffee Shop. Over lunch, Mark revealed his brainchild and John Fitzpatrick rolled his eyes toward heaven. But he agreed to broach the subject with the *Tribune* owners.

A series of subsequent discussions between the heads of Salt Lake City's two newspapers resulted in a warm friendship and mutual respect. Eventually the First Presidency and the Kearns family both granted guarded approval of the merger scheme, and details of the contract were hammered out.

The mills of the gods grind slowly but they grind exceeding fine. Congress had a mill too, and it ground to a halt. Under the Sherman Antitrust Act, the sharing of operations by two competing businesses was a *per se* violation in restraint of competition. However, aided by Paul H. Ray, founder of the Salt Lake law firm of Ray, Quinney, and Nebeker, with input from the Texas attorneys who had drawn up the Dallas agreement, the Newspaper Agency contract was prepared with John Fitzpatrick as president and Mark E. Petersen as vice-president. The amount of money to be saved on operations would be enormous. Still Congress dragged its feet.

President Clark, ever conscious of legal ramifications, felt that with the News Preservation Act (nicknamed the Crybaby Millionaire Relief Act) under consideration, it was safe to proceed. The Kearns family, who owned the *Tribune*, agreed. Many newspapers in the United States were owned by wealthy families who felt a public duty to maintain a high standard of quality news coverage. But when the choice became either to close the newspaper doors or bankrupt the family, often a great paper shut down operations. The owners felt sorrow at ceasing publication, hence the term Crybaby Millionaires. This act provided for the use of a common printing plant by two competing newspapers with the approval of the United States Attorney General. Congress recognized the problem, but would the legislators ever get around to making the law?

After the merger of the printing and mechanical operations of the two newspapers, Mark and John Fitzpatrick often found themselves flying to San Francisco to explain to the divisional head of the Justice Department the reason for their

violation of the antitrust statute. With Paul H. Ray representing them, the two would arrive at the airport in separate cars,
avoid speaking together before plane time, and generally re-
frain from any contact that would indicate to an onlooker
that together they spent their Mondays with the Department
of Justice—"like the Mafia," Mark said. Finally, at President
Clark's suggestion, Paul Ray traveled to Washington, D.C., in
pursuit of a favorable ruling. He managed to convince the
head of the Justice Department that unless the Newspaper
Agency Corporation contracts received government approval, two responsible newspapers, both vital to the community, would meet their deaths at the hands of the Sherman
Antitrust Act. His victory was important to the future of the
newspaper industry of the entire United States. Congres-
sional approval of the News Preservation Act was years away,
but when it became generally known that the Salt Lake Newspaper Agency contract had Justice Department approval,
newspapers all over the nation followed suit. The chorus of
protests against the antitrust restrictions finally led to the
passing of enabling legislation.

If Mark took pride in any accomplishment, the forming
of the Newspaper Agency Corporation was his choice. But he
was also aware that without support from Albert E. Bowen,
who could have killed the idea before he started; President J.
Reuben Clark, who shepherded the legal work; John Fitzpatrick and the *Tribune* owners, who fully cooperated; and Paul
H. Ray, who knew his law, the agency might still be a dream.

Another high point occurred when Mark completed
negotiations with the Chandler family, owners of the *Los
Angeles Times*, and the two papers jointly purchased a paper
mill, which guaranteed availability of newsprint even in the
event of a shortage. When the management of the *Deseret
News* decided later to trade its interest in the paper mill for
stock in the *Los Angeles Times*, Mark felt as if one of his children had been sold at auction. Having lived through the
shortages of paper in the Second World War and finding
himself in a position where he literally had to go on his

knees to owners of paper mills and beg for enough of their
product to put out a newspaper, he had vowed he would see
that the *News* owned its own source of newsprint. However,
he knew that it was no longer any of his business. With his
great ability to forget the things he could not change, he expressed his feelings to his family, then walked away.

Many years later Mark returned from an overseas trip and
found in his mail a long-forgotten article from *Time*
magazine dated March 20, 1950. His twin sister, Mona, had
found the clipping while sorting through her scrapbook. The
accompanying picture showed Mark with steady gaze and
coal-black hair, staring into the camera. The article stated,
"Though some Mormons may dislike the Deseret News' dog-
matism, that is nevertheless the reason for its success. The
official voice of the Church, the News is run by Editor and
General Manager Mark Edward Petersen, 49, who is also one
of the Twelve Apostles. A lean, intense and handsome man,
Petersen started out as a News cub at 20 and is still very much
a newsman; his staffers call him Mark instead of brother as is
customary with other high Church dignitaries.

"When he is not battling theological error at the University of Utah, Editor Petersen wages war against his powerful
competition, the morning Tribune and the evening Telegram. Both are owned by the family of the late mining king
and US Senator Thomas Kearns of Utah. In two years the
Mormon Church has invested about two million dollars in
expanding and improving the News, including a type-face
lifting.

"Under Editor Petersen, the News avoids cheesecake,
generally shies away from sensationalism, but is not above
reporting an occasional sex murder. As circulation builders
it uses giveaway contests with prizes as high as $50,000 in
cash. For non-Mormon readers the News also gives faithful
objective coverage to the news of other churches.

"In June the News will celebrate its centennial. The first
issue (circ. 225) reporting Terrible Fire In San Francisco
(which happened six months before) was edited by Willard

Richards, Prophet [Joseph] Smith's secretary. It was printed on presses shipped from the east; the early Latter-day Saints had paid the expenses by chipping in beans, hams and venison. Today's Latter-day Saints are still made to feel responsible for the paper's support. The church sends the paper free to a nonsubscribing Mormon for two weeks. Then, if the new reader wishes to cancel the subscription he is expected to notify Apostle Petersen first and give a good reason."

Mark subscribed to *Time* for years. In 1947 he had written a long letter to the editor objecting to their coverage of George Albert Smith in connection with the Pioneer Centennial. He received a reply acknowledging his corrections with vague apology for misuse of facts and inaccuracies but stating that the magazine provided its subscribers with interpretations that made for easy reading. Now with delight he pointed out to his family that *Time* had missed on the money amounts, the age at which he joined the *News* (he was still on his mission during his twentieth year), and especially on the calls from nonsubscribing Mormons that he allegedly received. He shuddered to think of the hours spent on the telephone that would result from such a rule. However, he objected not at all to being called "a lean, intense and handsome man and still very much a newsman."

During the 1950s, Mark embarked on another venture, one that was to give him great pleasure and sustain his interest for the rest of his life. This was the writing and publishing of books on gospel and scriptural subjects. His first book was *Your Faith and You*, a collection of Church editorials, which was published in October 1953. Shortly after, he was called into President Clark's office, congratulated on breaking into print, and reminded that he had already been paid for the editorials. The royalties should go to the *Deseret News*. The great love and respect Mark felt for President Clark compelled him to accept this suggestion, and he willingly donated his royalties to the paper. Six additional volumes of editorials were subsequently published over the years, with over 52,000 copies sold.

In 1962 *One Lord, One Faith* was published. This was a volume underlining Mark's belief that the teachings of the Savior were to be taken literally: "One Lord, one faith, and one baptism." Although the book was not a great commercial success, it was one of Mark's favorites.

Often Mark wrote in response to a definite need he observed. When members of the Church of Christ and the Jehovah's Witnesses caused difficulties for Latter-day Saint missionaries, Mark wrote two tracts, "Christ, Jehovah and 'The Witnesses'" and "Peter and the Rock." His book *As Translated Correctly* further answered questions arising from these two groups.

During his rare leisure hours on Diestel Road, Mark wrote *The Way of the Master*. As a reporter in 1932, he had covered a story on a man who announced the world would end in 1937. It seemed only logical to go on to study polygamists, dream-mine advocates, the Church of the Firstborn, and various other groups whose common denominator was their belief that the Church had gone astray. Mark found many good qualities in most of the members of these organizations, but he felt that their leadership was extremely misguided. He hoped that *The Way of the Master* might convince some of his "clients," as he called them, to reconsider the source of plural marriage. He was pleased when the First Presidency ordered a special edition of 5,000 copies to be sent to all the bishops and stake presidents in western America and wherever the polygamists might be.

When a group of polygamists published a book on the so-called Adam-God theory, which was so abhorrent to Mark, his immediate reaction was to write his own book on the subject. He felt that anyone who studied the scriptures should understand that Adam was Michael and that Christ was the firstborn and only begotten Jehovah. *Adam: Who Is He?* answered any questions that might arise and became the first in a series of books on the Old Testament, a true labor of love on Mark's part.

For years, almost every young person in the Church received a copy of Mark's little volume *For Time or Eternity* as an introduction to the temple. Looking toward the bicentennial of the United States, he wrote *The Great Prologue*, probably his most widely read book. The dedication of this work states, "To the latter-day ministry of the Lord Jesus Christ, for whose glorious second coming we eagerly wait; To the sacred memory of the Prophet Joseph Smith, the Lord's anointed restorer of latter days, who, by the grace of our Savior, laid the foundation for the establishment of the kingdom of God in these times; To the Patriots of '76 who lived and fought and died for the liberties we now enjoy under an inspired Constitution and a star-spangled flag of the free in this great land which is choice above all other lands."

From the time Mark went to work at the *Deseret News*, his typing speed had been legendary. Although he never adjusted to an electric machine, he typed faster than most secretaries and literally destroyed a typewriter every two or three years. When his family sweetly asked why he purchased each new typewriter, knowing very well how he could beat a machine to death, he replied with equal candor that he guessed it just wore out. Whether working on a speaking assignment or a pageant, writing editorials, or preparing a new book, Mark rolled the paper into his typewriter with a flourish and began attacking the keys. Someone said that he had his own type system. This was not so. He painstakingly taught himself to type by touch. Emma used to say that he typed as fast as she drove.

When he began a book, Mark usually went through ten or twelve sheets of paper before he composed an introduction that pleased him. As he typed and it became apparent that a new start was necessary, he pulled the paper from the roller, scrunched it into a ball, and threw it on the floor. The number of papers discarded across the carpet allowed anyone who dared approach at this critical time to see his approximate rate of progress on the book.

When his secretary, Dorene, first worked on a manuscript for him, she was surprised that after the book was finished and a large quantity of the paper he had purchased remained, he asked her to put this paper with the regular church supplies to help "pay for the wear and tear on the typewriter." Another action of Mark's that amazed his family was that he estimated the value of the gifts he received for birthdays and Christmas and paid tithing on them. When he came to live with Peggy's family and for the first time they became aware that this was his practice, they queried his reasoning. He explained that gifts were an increase, and one must tithe one's increase.

When Mark was approached by a fledgling author for help in publishing her work, he did all he could to put her in touch with the right people. After her manuscript was accepted and published, Peggy read the book and then told her father that she thought it was poorly written. With a mischievous smile, Mark replied, "If you think the book is bad now, you should have read it before I rewrote it." This was typical of his kindness in helping young people break into the book business.

Mark wrote prodigiously in every spare moment. Once, while on a Church assignment in Australia, he discovered that he had a free Friday. He immediately borrowed a typewriter and began a new book, *The Unknown God*. In one day he wrote the first twenty pages and outlined the rest of the manuscript. Two new books waited on Mark's desk when he returned from Australia—*Moses, Man of Miracles* and *Marriage, Covenants and Conflicts*. The Moses book was written because he felt that so many people were trying to dispute the Bible. In the marriage book, he quoted from Sister Camilla Kimball and Sister Belle Spafford, both of whom he considered extremely brilliant women.

With the appearance of his book *Those Gold Plates*, Mark declared to the world that "the gold plates given to the Prophet Joseph Smith for the translation of the Book of Mormon were genuine, real and authentic. They were as real as the gold plates found recently in Korea. They were as real as the gold and silver plates found in the ruins of the palace of

*Mark and
Emma Marr*

King Darius of ancient Persia. They were as real as the gold, silver and magnesium carbonate plates of Sargon II of Assyria. They were as real as the gold plates found at Pyrgi in Italy, and as genuine as any of the other Etruscan artifacts discovered in the area." He went on to list copper plates discovered with the Dead Sea Scrolls, silver plates from India, copper plates in the Pali language, the single sheet engraved on gold from Central Java, and concluded, "The gold plates of the Book of Mormon were just as real as those of Sargon, Darius, the Etruscans, the Essenes, or any others left by the ancients."

A red-letter day for Mark was the day when two new books came off the press—*Abraham, Friend of God* was published by Deseret Book, and *The Forerunners*, published by Bookcraft. Each of the volumes in his Old Testament series depicted a man's face under the title, then "Mark E. Petersen."

One of the proposed covers for the Abraham book pictured a very old, very bent man, with "Mark E. Petersen" written across his chest. Mark hung this picture on the refrigerator with the caption "My latest portrait." *The Forerunners* compared the lives and missions of Joseph Smith and John the Baptist in preparing for the coming of Christ. When she was in junior high, Peggy had started writing for her school newspaper and exhibiting an interest in a journalistic career, so Mark taught her the things he thought important. One of the most prolific writers in the Church at that time always gave Mark a copy of his new books, which were basically compilations of other peoples' work, and Mark once pointed out how little of the copy came from the pen of the author. One of his teachings was, "Never write with scissors like this man." With the publication of *The Forerunners*, Peggy was able to tease her father-mentor, for she had written a book, *John the Baptist*, and *The Forerunners* of necessity used many of the same scriptural references. She told her father that she hoped that never again would he write with his scissors.

Another of his Old Testament books was *Joseph of Egypt*, which follows through to the modern-day Joseph, Joseph Smith. Mark wrote in his journal, "I have had a desire to do this for some time but now feel pushed to do it." This book made its debut with Johnny, his first great-grandchild. When Johnny's mother brought the baby to the Church Office Building cafeteria for lunch with him, Mark held Johnny up for all to see and announced, "Everybody, look at my first great-grandchild!"

His book *Three Kings of Israel*, which dealt with Saul, David, and Solomon, was a pleasure to write. The fall from greatness of these three powerful men who yielded to temptation when they were at the pinnacle of their lives always reminded Mark of President Clark's hope that he might be able to endure to the end. Peggy who went through Mark's manuscripts for repeated words, phrasing, and grammar, asked her father why so few changes were needed in this particular volume. He replied that the book had written itself.

When Mark's book *Isaiah for Today* appeared, he was sure that it would do well for two reasons: the general fascination of most Latter-day Saints for Isaiah and his prophecies and the fact that the book's profits went to the missionary fund. He told Peggy that if she wanted to write a best seller, she should donate the royalties to the missionaries, just as her mother had done. Emma Marr had been a prolific writer, the author of several books for youth. After her death, as Mark received royalty checks for her books, he sent them to the Church missionary fund according to her wishes. He was pleased to note that her publications made more money than his even though she was no longer alive. Emma Marr's fervent love of the missionary system and the bittersweet memories of her own conversion convinced her that nothing could be purchased with money that would rival the value received from missionary donations. She always paid her tithing and fast offerings with love and gratitude for the kind Father in heaven who allowed her to keep nine-tenths of the abundance she enjoyed. But somehow the money she donated to the missionaries pleased her even more, and Mark delighted in continuing this tradition.

Mark continued to write almost to the day he died, and several of his books were published posthumously. These volumes, including two on the Book of Mormon and one on the teachings of Paul, were written despite great physical discomfort. He had been undergoing radiation treatments, and one effect of the treatments was extreme dryness of his hands. As he typed, his fingers split and bled. He tried a variety of creams and lotions and finally in disgust covered his fingertips with adhesive tape as a protection. Those close to him cannot see any of those last books without remembering his poor painful hands.

Delighted that Emma Marr's books on the Bible had continued to sell long after her death, Mark felt that a small, inexpensive volume of Bible stories should be kept next to the bed of every child in the Church. Thus he wrote *How The Rainbow Came and Other Bible Stories*, the last of his more than fourscore books.

In addition to his many books, Mark wrote editorials for the *Church News*, beginning in the 1930s and continuing until his death. If he had to be away from home on Church assignments, he would write enough editorials to cover the time away. When he died in January 1984, he had left enough editorials to go partly through March. It has been estimated that he wrote some 5,200 editorials, many of which were compiled in book form.

Why does any author write forty-three books? What drew Mark to his typewriter night after night and on his Mondays off? Each of his books was a statement of his beliefs, an answer to questions from within the Church, a need seen. He was embarrassed at the number of volumes. When with a family member he walked from his office across South Temple to Deseret Book to see how his latest writing fared, he was horrified at the long row of his works on the shelf. He always said, "No one has that much to say. I definitely will not write another book." This phase usually lasted a month at most; then either a question arising in a conference or something in his constant reading triggered an idea, and once again the sound of his typewriter echoed in the back of the house. Sheepishly he would produce a first chapter or an outline and ask for an evaluation of his latest idea. The crumpled balls of discarded paper rolled across the carpet, the keys clattered, and he was on his way. Only his death could still his pen.

10

The West European Mission

"As a man travelling into a far country"
(Matthew 25:14)

Mark had been involved with dispensing Church information since his call to the Twelve. Whenever publicity or news releases were needed, he was their man. In 1955 he received an assignment to precede the Tabernacle Choir on its grand European concert tour to Scotland, England, Wales, Denmark, Germany, The Netherlands, Switzerland, and France. With several stops in each of these countries, the trip required expert help and much preparation.

Robert Mullen, who was considered one of the great public relations men in the United States, was asked to travel with Mark. They would arrange for advance publicity and make necessary reservations to guarantee a successful concert tour. Mark had never before been to Europe, and when Bob Mullen proved to be so comfortable a companion, he was sure that the trip would be easy, enjoyable, and enlightening. Easy and enjoyable it was not; enlightening it certainly was.

In London, the first stop, Mr. Mullen developed a severe case of flu and could not raise his head from the pillow, leaving Mark—an innocent abroad if ever there was one—to book hotels, meet the media, and generally pave the way for the movement of hundreds of people across a continent as strange to him as darkest Africa. Happily his newspaper training carried him through, and the experience proved one of his favorite times. Discovering that there is nothing like a case of the flu to cement a friendship, Robert Mullen and

Mark, along with Elder Richard L. Evans, worked with great
relish on future projects for Church information.

As President McKay expanded the scope of the Church,
he embarked on a great temple-building program. When the
entire Council of the Twelve was invited to the dedication of
the Los Angeles Temple, Mark and Matthew Cowley decided
to travel together with their wives on the train to California.
The trip there was especially pleasant because Emma and
Sister Cowley had become close friends, and the foursome
traded anecdotes as the miles flew by. None of them realized
that this was to be the last occasion they would share, for at
the cornerstone-laying ceremony Elder Cowley became ill,
and he died shortly thereafter. His death left a void for Mark,
who had loved Matt Cowley's strong testimony and keen wit
as they shared experiences as junior members of the Twelve.

For two months Mark and Emma traveled south of the
border, touring missions and holding meetings with members, missionaries, and investigators. Emma played the piano
and organ and spoke from the pulpit, telling of her conversion and the love she felt for the missionary program. Mark
with his Bible gave all the reasons for the Restoration, explaining the marks of identification of the true church. When
his audience grew tired, he would ask them to stand and sing
a song or recite a scripture. With gentle persuasion, he challenged investigators to be baptized and the members to
search the scriptures.

Mark, who had declared that he would rather be a newspaperman than anything else in the world, discovered that
he would rather be a Special Witness than anything else in
the world. With his Emma Marr, he found a satisfaction and
joy in his Church travels never before experienced by either
of them. They were quite a team, and they looked forward to
each new assignment.

Sent to tour the Hawaiian Mission and dedicate the
Kahala Ward meetinghouse, Mark and Emma were particu-
larly delighted, for the mission president was D. Arthur
Haycock, treasurer of the *Deseret News* and longtime friend

*Mark and
Emma Marr*

and associate. Mark wrote, "He carried on an excellent and outstanding administration. He was well loved by the people and very valuable because he could speak the native tongue as well as the natives themselves, and they loved it."

What had been an impossible dream in 1920 became reality when Mark was assigned to break ground for the first Latter-day Saint chapel in Dartmouth, Nova Scotia. His feelings almost overwhelmed him when he turned the first shovel of earth, and he spoke with great emotion of the street meetings he had conducted as a young elder in Dartmouth.

Mark and Emma congratulated themselves on their unbelievable good luck when they were assigned to accompany President and Sister McKay on a tour of the Northern and Southern Far East missions. When the time came to leave, President McKay's health prevented his making the trip, so the Petersens took off on their own. At that time, the total Church membership in Japan was only 2,282 in 25 branches. An auditorium in Tokyo filled with 750 Saints seemed an enormous crowd. In Korea 410 people had joined the Church, and no one imagined that a temple might be required in the future. Okinawa boasted 111 members, while Manila had a group of 120 LDS servicemen.

When Mark and Emma arrived in Toronto to create the three hundredth stake in his former mission headquarters, they also toured the Canadian Mission, then presided over by President Thomas S. Monson. After the historic event marking stake number 300, what could be more pleasant than to see the results of the labors of Tom and Frances Monson, both of whom had come to work at the *News* when Mark was manager and they were teenagers. In his early twenties Thomas Monson became the youngest bishop in the Church, and Mark couldn't have been more proud had he been his own son.

As Mark examined the mission records and saw that President Monson had motivated his missionaries to increase their baptisms, he was pleased. But his greatest satisfaction came from discovering that the increased baptisms were all high-quality, true conversions. Remembering the admonition that "your fruit should remain," President Monson was on his way to converting all of Canada. Again Mark could not have felt more pride and joy if Tom had been his own flesh and blood.

The Petersens and Monsons traveled from branch to branch by car, and whenever Mark and Emma traveled by car, they sang. The Monsons found themselves humming obscure hymns they hadn't heard in years—and all the verses of all the hymns. Emma Marr's phenomenal memory for words of songs had rescued many soloists for whom she had played accompaniments. Now she coached the Monsons whenever a blank appeared.

A strong bond forged by association as newspapermen and reinforced by Church commitment drew Thomas S. Monson and Mark E. Petersen together. They might joke about whether names spelled with "son" were superior to names spelled with "sen," or consider the merits of Danes and Swedes. But regardless of ancestry, they were brothers, their ties deepening with the years. And Mark and Emma felt that in Frances, Tom had found the perfect partner.

In Canada, as on all his mission tours, Mark challenged his listeners to become Saints, to be baptized, to study the life of Christ, to learn of Him. His earnest testimony and his love of the Savior helped him communicate with the fence-sitters, many of whom made a commitment to the Church after hearing him speak. Still remembering his experiences as a young elder, he knew that he could never prepare a talk in advance when working with investigators. Inspiration and his scriptures led the way as he built his case for the true gospel.

When President Clark developed health problems that prevented his getting around easily, Mark found himself visiting him at home whenever he had not seen him at the office. In these private conversations the great churchman-statesman-attorney continued to teach Mark on a variety of subjects, teachings often fondly recalled. In later life Mark had little patience with people who thought they were so good that no improvement could be made in their beliefs or behavior. He felt that J. Reuben Clark was one of the most dedicated men who had ever lived upon the earth, and on his deathbed President Clark had taught Mark the ultimate lesson. Knowing that he would die soon, he clutched Mark's hand and said, over and over again, "I hope that I will endure to the end." Mark felt that if President Clark, who had lived the greatest of lives, needed to worry about enduring to the end, other members of the human race should continue to work out their salvation and never rest on their laurels or think their place in the hereafter had been made sure. When President Clark died, Mark knew he had lost a dear friend. From Mark's first appearance at 47 East South Temple as a church reporter, President Clark had singled him out, demanding excellence in all he did and providing oppor-

Mark and President J. Reuben Clark

tunities to grow. His passing left a void, and for months when the phone rang at the office, out of habit Mark wondered if it were President Clark.

Whenever Mark received an appointment for which he had great enthusiasm, it seemed destined to be short-lived. President McKay suggested that he accept a position on the board of trustees of Weber College in Ogden, Utah. Mark was delighted. He joined the board in April 1962. In December of that year, President McKay again approached him, this time following a Church employees' Christmas party, and asked him to wait until everyone else had left. Mark's relationship with President McKay was especially warm, and he waited without worry as the Prophet greeted the last of the crowd.

When President McKay suggested Mark might like to sit down, he still felt no particular apprehension. But the news that Mark and Emma were to take charge of the West European missions came as a shock. This involved all of Europe except the Scandinavian and German-speaking countries, plus the servicemen in the Mediterranean, Nigeria, and West

Central Africa (a total of eleven missions). Even more exciting was the announcement that they had only two weeks to
get ready. They were to arrive in England January 14, 1963.
Mark resigned from the Weber College board with regret.

On December 26, 1962, Mark was formally appointed
president of the West European Mission, succeeding President N. Eldon Tanner. Nineteen days later he and Emma
emerged from a British Airways plane to be greeted by President Marion D. Hanks of the British Mission. Sharing mutual
affection and admiration, Mark and President Hanks understood each other, and with the presence of Elder Hanks's
wife, Maxine, and his children, the Petersens felt not at all
alone. President Hanks retrieved their luggage and drove
them to White Hayes, Givons Grove, Leatherhead, Surrey,
England, their home for the next three years. Europe was experiencing the worst winter in two centuries. Ice jammed
harbors, and ships unable to discharge or pick up cargo rode
at anchor in the distance. Transportation of all kinds was dis-
rupted, and Londoners shivered under layers of heavy clothing.

Until she was fifteen Emma had lived in Liverpool, England, and she should have remembered how piercing the
moist cold winters could be. Over the years, American central heating had dimmed this memory, however, and the almost unbearable chill came as a surprise. Even less welcome
was the discovery that all the power was off at White Hayes—
no heat, no lights. And darkness arrived by four o'clock in
Leatherhead in the winter. However, from what could be
seen of the house, it was more than pleasant. The baby grand
in the living room caught Emma's eye. Mark found the office
and pronounced it perfect.

Rapid expansion of the Church brought to England a
group of building personnel, who were living in the next village. President Hanks called one of them to turn on the
power. With lights and heat, the Petersens examined their
new surroundings, then collapsed in bed. When they awoke,
the house was colder than ever. They were to wear their

coats inside and out-of-doors for the next five months. Mark learned to turn the pages of his scriptures with gloved fingers, and Emma discovered the British stronghold of Marks and Spencers stores, where she bought several pairs of woolen underwear that, worn one on top of the other, added to her bulk and her comfort.

The weather was insignificant compared to President McKay's reason for sending Mark to Europe. In Mark's own words, "There were two outstanding problems in connection with the work in the West European Mission. One was the proselyting program by which 'baseball baptisms' were being made whereby youngsters were baptized into the Church without any instruction and sometimes without the knowledge or consent of their parents. Under President McKay's instructions, we were to discontinue such things and bring the missions back to a normal proselyting program.

"The second major item was the high cost of building LDS chapels over there. Building supervisors from America were sent to construct chapels with the assistance of locally called young men in England serving as laborers. One building supervisor and the two young men assigned to each job did all of the work, which, of course, was supervised by other men in the building department who were located in the building offices in Epsom."

Four very capable men had been called as presidents in the West European missions: David B. Haight in Scotland, Ray Curtis and Phil D. Jensen in England, and, of course, Marion D. Hanks in London. Mark asked these men to form a committee to prepare a series of six door approaches, which he would have printed and distributed to the missionaries to use as they went tracting. If one door approach was not accepted by the people, the elders were to switch to an alternative one, making every effort to engage in gospel conversation. Regular proselyting went on from that time forward.

The immediate effect of this move was a drop in baptisms. However, with strong support from the mission presidents, Mark was able to convert the missionaries to baptisms based on teaching and conversion through the Spirit. As a result of this new program, those who were baptized had testimony of the gospel and provided strength to the wards and branches.

After aiming the missions in the right direction, Mark felt that the building program needed radical changes. He made a study of building costs of schools and churches in England. Through an organization of British architects in London, he obtained drawings and prices for steel, concrete, and brick schools and for beautiful British churches. He submitted his reports to the First Presidency with the recommendation that more local materials and designs be used. He was alarmed at the expensive and sometimes inferior materials being shipped from the United States when more appropriate high-quality supplies were available locally. He also had the feeling that some of the workers involved didn't know which end of a hammer to use. Mark understood carpentry. But no one at home seemed very excited about his findings until the roof of one of the new chapels collapsed. His point was well taken. The First Presidency made a change in the building program.

Mark discovered that Church books imported from the United States were too costly for many of the members, so he began having the scriptures printed locally at a much reduced cost. Occasionally a new convert would join the Church and then, hearing of some event in the past, want to disassociate himself as a member. Mark wanted the people to understand the history of the Church before they became members. Elder Gordon B. Hinckley had written an excellent history of the Church, and Mark sent a letter to the First Presidency asking permission to condense and publish the book in England so that it could be sold for a dollar. Then he insisted that before anyone was baptized, the prospective convert read this little volume, now called *Truth Restored,* and attend enough meetings to feel comfortable with the members. By the time the convert was baptized, he would have a complete overview of the organization.

Amid general grumbling about all the new rules and regulations, the missionaries discovered that the system worked! The converts who joined the Church remained in the fold. Mark's emphasis on baptizing families provided much-needed leadership and stability in the branches. And the baptism rate, which had fallen drastically low, began to climb. With the help of the mission presidents, Mark wrote seven missionary lessons to be given before baptism. Then, feeling inspired to add to the program, he composed a tract now used Churchwide called "After Baptism What?" Seven more lessons to be delivered after baptism followed. Combined with a reading of the Book of Mormon and *Truth Restored*, the converts had a Ph.D. in Mormonism. And the fruit remained.

Mark decided to send the missionaries to contact all inactive members. He hoped to receive invitations to reteach the gospel. While working with the inactives, the missionaries invited family members to listen to the lessons. Seventy-five percent of those contacted in this way were reactivated, and many baptisms resulted in their families. And the fruit remained.

With growing membership, Mark wondered how he could train branch members and still leave time for the missionaries to proselyte. He contacted the Missionary Committee in Salt Lake City and asked them to send him more couples. Older men and women with experience in the Church could live within the boundaries of a branch or ward and draw on their first-hand knowledge in training the new members. Mark wrote in his journal, "The older couples are going into wards and branches, working among the inactives and giving leadership. They have performed miracles in training and reclaiming members."

Having convinced the First Presidency that the building program needed radical modification, Mark found that he could build many more buildings with less money. By using local talent, plans, and materials to construct chapels that would do credit to any part of the Church, Mormons gained widespread recognition as the group who built "that beautiful little church down the street." By the end of his first year, twenty-two new buildings were in use, and twenty more were completed the next year. During 1964, he would oversee the start of forty other buildings in his eleven missions.

As more chapels were constructed in the British missions, Mark thought that a perfect way to become acquainted with the people of the area would be to hold open houses in the chapels, present a musical program, and serve refreshments. Any false notions about the ordinances performed and activities held in the buildings were immediately forgotten as neighbors walked from room to room. Investigators in particular were urged to attend these open houses, and many baptisms resulted.

As the head of the West European Mission, Mark was responsible for the United States servicemen's units in Western Europe and throughout the Mediterranean. Visits to camps in Turkey, Libya, Greece, and Cypress became the rule, as well as travel to bases in England, France, Belgium, The Netherlands, and Spain. Mark and Emma thrived on these travels, enjoying their servicemen's contacts and bringing to the service families the feeling of home. Captain John Lasater, who was stationed at Orleans in France, acted as servicemen's coordinator and general guide. It was Captain Lasater who discovered Emma's passion for shopping and arranged some remarkable trips in out-of-the-way places. While Mark conducted Church interviews, Emma and the Captain made the rounds of shops and bazaars.

As Mark and Emma toured their missions, they demonstrated door approaches and methods to the missionaries. Mark played the elder and Emma the housewife. Emma delighted in giving her missionary as difficult a time as possible, and general laughter usually resulted. But as the elders watched their president respond to his witty wife, they felt that they also could meet with aplomb any problem that arose.

When Mark taught the missionaries, he used a chalkboard to list references from the scriptures as well as outlines for lessons and door approaches. He relied heavily on audience participation and loved to call a sleepy elder to the front of the room to demonstrate a hypothetical situation. Mark's natural good humor and optimism carried his enthusiastic listeners along. He asked for audience recitation of scriptures, and if the missionaries responded in a quiet way or not at all, he tried to help them realize that they could not teach principles they themselves didn't understand. His own missionary experiences came rushing back. He had felt discouragement, and he knew what it meant never to baptize.

A highlight of the Petersens' European stay was the visit of President David O. McKay to dedicate the Merthyr Tydfil chapel in Wales. President McKay's mother was born within a block of the new building. President McKay was thrilled when two sessions each with 1,300 persons in attendance were held, and the Saints and investigators were impressed.

Mark was delighted when a missionary discovered that the building President McKay had mentioned as changing the direction of his first mission was being demolished. As a young elder, David O. McKay had been tracting and wondering what he was doing on a mission when he passed an old building and read on the capstone of an arch, "What e're thou art, act well they part." President McKay had taken this as a sign that he should remain in the field and do his part well, and his entire missionary experience improved dramatically from that time forward. A sharp missionary asked the builders for the arch, and Mark was able to have it shipped to Salt Lake City, where it was put on display.

Shortly after President McKay's visit, Mark developed a health problem. He had heard stories from the elders about the nationalized health system, but he thought they probably were exaggerated. Supposedly there were only two kinds of pills, and regardless of disease or broken bones, the patient got yellow or white. If one was given both, it was time to look for a burial plot. Mark called a clinic for an appointment. By the time he saw the doctor the next day, he was terribly uncomfortable. But he was not so uncomfortable that he failed to notice the dust on the floor of the waiting room and the tea stains and cigarette ashes down the front of the nurse's uniform. Throughout his life, Mark was prepared to like the people he met and think the best of professionals he contacted, but even he was concerned at the unsanitary conditions in the office. When Mark explained what was ailing him, the doctor said, "You must see a specialist. I will make an appointment for you." He disappeared into an adjoining room, then returned and joyfully announced that the specialist could see Mark in just three weeks. When Mark explained that under the circumstances he could not wait three weeks, the doctor cluck-clucked about American impatience.

Returning to White Hayes, Mark called his physician in Salt Lake City and was told to get on the next plane. Blessing Marion D. Hanks for being in place to take over duties of the

White Hayes, the mission home in England

West European missions, Mark and Emma flew from London to Chicago. Pan Am had a physician waiting at the Chicago airport, and after brief treatment, the Petersens continued to Salt Lake City. Minor surgery and a vein operation in his leg followed; then Mark was able to meet with President McKay and report to him on the missionary programs in Europe.

Mark felt that his health problem was providential, for it allowed him to hear President McKay explain a little more about the reason for his overseas assignment. President McKay told him that he had been ill and thought he was dying. Then he dreamed that he had gone to the other side and that all his family there were preparing a happy reunion for him. But just as he reached his arms toward his waiting relatives, a voice said to him that his time had not come, for he had work still to do. President McKay felt a deep conviction that it was Mark Petersen who must go abroad. Mark was humbled by the story and vowed to give all his energy for the work of the Lord.

After a few weeks, the Petersens returned to White Hayes and were surprised to discover that it seemed like home. White Hayes, a large house, had an apartment where the two elders who served as mission secretaries lived. These young men became like sons to Mark and Emma, keeping in touch with them long after their missions were completed. Universally the elders remember the great courtesy Mark showed to his wife, always rising when she entered a room, holding her chair at mealtime, opening car doors, showing concern.

One of the first secretaries, Perry Driggs, had come into the field fresh from an engineering degree at Massachusetts Institute of Technology and an MBA from Harvard. Mark, never afraid to delegate to a capable assistant, used Elder Driggs to set up the printing business that became so important to the European Saints. Long before the Petersen era, a fleet of Jaguars had been purchased for the mission presidents in England. These cars were extremely impressive to look at but expensive and mechanically unsatisfactory. Elder Driggs needed both his engineering and business educations to keep Mark's car operating. One of Mark's first points of business was to dispose of the Jaguars and substitute more reliable automobiles.

When the Petersens' daughter Peggy came for a visit with her three children, ages seven, nine, and eleven, Elder Driggs received a new claim to fame. Mark, the eleven-year-old, followed the elders interminably, asking questions constantly. When he wasn't with the elders, he gently harassed his two younger sisters, Sydney and Drew. Sydney and Drew found neighbor girls to play with, often on the balcony above the first floor. One day Mark discovered that the door to the balcony could be locked; a key conveniently waited for this purpose. When the little girls began to play, he quietly locked the door, stranding them on the balcony. He then pocketed the key and disappeared. The neighbor children were called home for lunch, but no means could be found to release them from their prison. Eventually Mark and the key appeared, but Elder Driggs had had enough. When Peggy returned with her mother, she found Mark spreadeagled on the back lawn, held securely by croquet hoops placed by Perry Driggs. The elder immediately became the hero of Sydney and Drew.

Another favorite secretary was Hyrum Wayne Smith. Elder Smith had a way with words and an irresistible twinkle in his eye. When President Hugh B. Brown came to tour the missions, a banquet in his honor found Elder Smith as master of ceremonies. President Brown was so overcome with mirth at Elder Smith's comments that the elders worried that they might have to carry him out. Elder Smith had a special place in Emma's affections. When Mark traveled the missions, occasionally she chose to stay home. As soon as her husband was safely deposited at the airport she would call, "Elder Smith, what movie are we going to see tonight?"

The village of Leatherhead gave great pleasure to the Petersens and their secretaries, with a petrol station boasting a thatched roof, shops from a Dickens novel, and a quaint pub (restaurant variety) that had to be seen to be believed.

When Emma heard the neighbors speaking of the frozen man, she imagined a polar apparition similar to Big Foot. In reality he was a sweet little person who brought packaged frozen foods door to door. And rabbit ears, a favorite sweet in the district, proved to be an ice cream cone with two sticks of Cadbury chocolate placed like ears on either side of the scoop. The quality of the clothing offered for sale pleased Mark and Emma, both of whom brought back to Utah sweaters that lasted the rest of their lives. The trains and buses performed so well that Mark could not understand why America had not adopted British methods of mass transportation.

Because she had lived in Liverpool during her growing-up years, Emma felt comfortable with things and people European. Because he regarded his wife as English, Mark was prejudiced in favor of those with whom he worked. The language, however, proved a stumbling block to him. He was misunderstood often. One day he and Emma drove to a meeting in a nearby town. Elder Driggs had explained that the chapel was next to the train station, but Mark drove around the village for a few minutes without finding any trains. Finally he asked a passerby the location of the train station. The man said he did not know. Mark stopped a bobby who was directing traffic. Did he know where the train station was? The bobby shook his head no. Mark braked at the petrol station. Could they show him the way to the trains? Another negative response. In desperation he returned to the bobby and said, "Could you please direct me to the tryne stytion." "Why didn't you sye so?" said the bobby, pointing the way to go.

The most moving factor in Mark's mission presidency was his gift of the Spirit. When President Hugh B. Brown visited the West European missions, he called a meeting of the eleven mission presidents. At one session, when Mark had left the room to make arrangements for lunch, President Brown confided to the group, "You have been very fortunate to have spent three years of your lives with Elder Mark E. Petersen. None of you know the role Elder Petersen will play in the hereafter, but I tell you that it is a very important part." Mark returned to the meeting and the subject was dropped.

Mark and Emma traveled from mission to mission holding workshops, interviewing elders, visiting with the Saints, and conducting investigator gatherings. It was particularly at the investigator meetings that Mark came into his own. He so loved the gospel and wanted to share his testimony of the mission of the Savior that his voice would swell with emotion. When he looked an audience in the eyes and declared in his resonant voice, "I know," no one questioned his knowledge or sincerity. He used his Bible as a springboard and insisted on going from the known to the unknown, from the milk to the meat. As he shared his reasons for his testimony, always making each point with the help of a Bible scripture, the strength of his belief mesmerized his listeners. After the meetings, many of the investigators asked for baptism. Always Mark knew that the Spirit had touched him and touched the audience. His usual reply to Emma's comment on how wonderful his talk had been was, "I had a lot of help."

11

Richard L. Evans

"Why shouldst thou die before thy time?"
(Ecclesiastes 7:17)

In the summer of 1965, the First Presidency decided that members of the Twelve should not be stationed for long periods away from the headquarters of the Church. While Mark was in England, Elder Ezra Taft Benson presided over the European Mission with headquarters in Frankfurt. The First Presidency called them both home, retaining them as area supervisors for the next three years. Mark and Emma sailed for America on the *S.S. United States* in September 1965.

Upon his return from Europe, Mark was assigned to the Church Information Committee with Elders Richard L. Evans and Gordon B. Hinckley. The visitors' centers were included in this assignment. (The name of the Church Information Service was changed to the Public Communications Department in August 1972.) Mark had long been close to the two other men who carried the responsibility for information for the Church, and he was pleased to work with them. He had taught Gordon Hinckley as a child in the First Ward, and the youth had delivered Mark and Emma's newspaper. Richard Evans and Mark, occasionally called the two bad boys of the Twelve, shared a sometimes uncontrollable sense of humor. Nothing made them happier than to rewrite and restage one of the Church's pageants. When they worked together, it was always behind closed doors so that any hand clapping, back slapping, and laughter would not be misunderstood by visitors to the Church Administration Building.

Elder Evans often reminded Mark of the April 1950 gen-

*Mark and Ezra Taft Benson (back to camera) greet President
Stephen L Richards and President David O. McKay at general conference*

eral conference when they were scheduled to give the last
two talks. The earlier speakers in the session had run over-
time, leaving time for either Mark's or Elder Evans's speech,
but not both. Mark's admiration for Richard Evans's spoken
words knew no bounds. Putting his own prepared talk aside,
he rose and gave an extemporaneous three-minute gem on
perfection. This talk produced an overwhelming reaction in
its favor. Letters from all over the Church, from most of the
General Authorities, including President McKay, and from
radio listeners in many places flooded his office for a month.
Mark's intention had been only to give his dear Richard the
time, not create an uproar. And dear Richard always accused
him of making him give a talk while Mark had gotten out of
his.

Before David O. McKay had become president, none of

the General Authorities knew in advance when they were to speak in general conference. Each man sat listening intently to see whose name was read and, if someone else was called, took a deep breath of relief until the next announcement. By the last session of the third day, those who had not spoken were exhausted with the waiting. President McKay, who in the past had also listened anxiously for his name, decided that he would end the torture. He began scheduling the talks, notifying each person when and how long he would speak. The General Authorities appreciated this consideration, but occasionally someone failed to time his talk, or spoke extemporaneously and ignored the clock, and the last speaker sometimes found himself, like Mark, bearing his testimony and nothing more.

Mark's assignment to Church Information allowed him to implement many of his ideas for preaching the gospel. He believed in the soft sell, but he felt equally strongly that information must be disseminated. He was sure that an effective visitors' center where the story of the Church was told could provide the missionaries with almost all the referrals they could handle. Thus began his great career in advertising, decorating, broadcasting, drama, art, and script writing. Every July when General Authorities had no conference assignments, Mark and Emma traveled from one visitor's center to another, evaluating the displays, the presentations, the guides, and the atmosphere.

Mark's secretary, Dorene, knew that during July she should sit next to her phone, because her boss inevitably called to dictate a new script to help sell the gospel he so loved. Under his guidance, a network of visitors' centers covered the globe and reached out to those who sought the truth. At world's fairs and major expositions of all kinds, wherever a crowd of any magnitude gathered, a well-planned display manned by guides and missionaries met visitors and told them of the meaning of Christ's mission.

Mark originally planned the exhibits and the visitors' centers. He believed that when the scriptures said to take His

*Mark with
President Joseph
Fielding Smith*

yoke and learn of Him, they were to be interpreted literally.
He investigated the latest in dioramas and animation to present the story of the true church in its most appealing form.
Working with famous artists, he commissioned paintings of
sacred events. Hung in his office were two favorites, one of
Moroni burying the gold plates and the other of Mormon
writing the history of the Nephites, with some completed
records at his feet. When Richard L. Evans saw the latter painting, he pointed out to Mark that Mormon had some "footnotes."

If an inspection of a visitors' center revealed aging film-
strips, tattered posters, faded pictures, or disinterested
workers, Mark updated the materials, infused the staff with
enthusiasm, and generally moved whatever mountain stood
in the way of success. His testimony that the light of the gospel offered true happiness for all led him to think constantly
of new ways to tell the story of the Savior.

At Carthage, Illinois, he discovered that vandals had broken into the jail and destroyed mannequins representing

Joseph and Hyrum Smith. The Church Information Department had sent replacement mannequins, but the guides refused to use them, storing them in the attic of the jail. When
Mark climbed to the attic, he saw why. The heads on the mannequins looked nothing at all like the Prophet and his
brother. New heads were ordered, and a tape of Elder John
Longden singing "A Poor Wayfaring Man of Grief," which
John Taylor had sung at the martyrdom, completed the
exhibit. As he traveled the world, Mark kept an eye out for
couples who might be called to serve missions at visitors'
centers. He felt this to be one of the choice jobs in the Church.

From November 27 to December 12, 1965, Mark and
Emma toured the South African Mission. As they were so
close to the Holy Land, they decided to spend Christmas in
Jerusalem. When they arrived at their hotel on the Mount of
Olives, they were amazed to see Loren and Ila Wheelwright
standing nearby, admiring the view. Emma had become acquainted with Ila in Music Circle Club in Salt Lake City, and
Mark knew Loren through the printing business. Together
the four friends visited Shepherd's Field, Bethlehem, the
holy sites in Jerusalem, and Lazarus's Tomb, and traveled on
to Cairo. The pyramids held Mark spellbound as he visualized all the slaves who had lost their lives building them.
When he heard that a light show was scheduled that night
near the Sphinx, he insisted that they attend. The dramatic
lighting and fascinating script attracted hordes of tourists, reminding Mark of Salt Lake City in the summertime. As a
member of the Church Information Committee, he realized
that while Salt Lake City and vicinity offered all kinds of wonderful sights during the day, at night there was nothing for
the tourists except movies or the bars. He couldn't wait to return and see the expression on Richard Evans's face when he
proposed an outdoor light show. Instead of lights on the
Sphinx, they would light the temple.

Mark had enjoyed the centennial presentation of Crawford Gates's *Promised Valley* at the University of Utah. With
Richard Evans's help, he was sure they could stage an abbre-

viated version just behind 47 East South Temple, on the site that had been cleared for the plaza of the new high-rise Church Office Building, which was then in the planning stages. If the theater seats faced the temple, the temple lighting could be turned off until the finale and then, as a grand climax, the temple could be flooded with a blaze of lights as the tourists breathlessly watched. Crawford Gates gave his permission for a shortened version of his production, and the Brethren gave their permission for the location. The only thing left undone was to wait for good weather to build an outdoor theater.

The weather cooperated, a fine cast was assembled, and the tourists flocked to see the pioneer story and listen to the wonderful music while enjoying the evening air. Each night when, in the last scene, the formerly darkened temple burst into light, an audible gasp came from the 2,500 spectators.

Later, when construction of the high-rise building eliminated the theater site, Mark initiated a search for a building that could provide a home for *Promised Valley*. He began to spend his lunch hours strolling up and down the streets of downtown Salt Lake City, examining any property that might be adequately restored. Those who saw him perusing the less desirable locations in the city may have wondered at his choice of walking routes. Eventually the Lyric Theater, formerly the Orpheum Theater, seemed to him the only solution. Its faded elegance lay disguised beneath dirt and decay, adding little to the beauty of downtown Salt Lake City.

While Mark felt sad to lose the outdoor theater that had so successfully attracted the tourists, he saw the need for the high-rise office building taking its place. The Lyric, built in 1903, offered a satisfactory alternative. He convinced President Harold B. Lee that the theater was a necessary arm of the missionary effort. President Lee agreed, and the building was extensively renovated and christened the Promised Valley Playhouse.

Almost nightly during the outdoor run of *Promised Valley*, Mark and Emma had attended each performance, checking on the cast, the settings, and the effectiveness of the music and lighting. Now, as adviser to the Mutual Improvement Associations, Mark felt a duty to the youth of the Church to provide a training ground for developing talent. The Petersens were Broadway musical buffs, and Mark visualized the Promised Valley Playhouse providing uplifting entertainment for "the average wonderful little family who could not afford expensive entertainment." Because of the poverty in his own early married life, he was always concerned for those who had little money but great need for leisure-time activity.

In the new playhouse, the *Promised Valley* cast offered tourists two performances of the pioneer story nightly, and they played to packed houses. During the winter months musicals were imported from Brigham Young University, and local stakes also presented entertainment. It soon became apparent that the theater needed a staff and productions of its own and a permanent manager to direct its future. Ralph Rodgers, Jr., recently released as president of the Samoa Mission, accepted this position with instructions to plan high-class, high-calibre plays. He had first met Mark when he and his family had appeared in the outdoor production of *Promised Valley*.

Mark advised Ralph to "make Promised Valley Playhouse a training ground for the young inasmuch as the grand old days of the MIA have been done away with." June Conference and large-scale all-Church productions had been eliminated, and Mark was concerned that the Church was not producing a generation of performers, the crowning glory of the Church, as had been done in the past. In the Promised Valley Playhouse, aspiring artists could use their talents for the enjoyment of others while being trained by those with greater experience.

Mark visualized the playhouse as a musical theater. Between the newspaper business and some of his church counseling problems, he was always ready for a happy musical evening—light opera, Broadway shows, Gilbert and Sullivan, anything lovely. When Ralph Rodgers presented to the board the proposed plays for the coming year, he "was always amazed at how well Elder Petersen was versed in Broadway musicals." Mark felt that an exciting Broadway musical properly presented could bring the audience closer to the good life. According to Ralph, "He loved to go out of the theater whistling and happy and not depressed. He felt that through the arts, people could be attracted to the gospel. He was committed to individuals, wanting to reach out wherever he could. He attended every production at Promised Valley Playhouse while he was president of the board of directors."

As the future of the playhouse was evaluated, Mark began to talk about religious plays. Elder S. Dilworth Young's *The Long Road*, the story of the Prophet Joseph Smith, was worked over by Elder Young, Ralph Rodgers, and Mark, and presented to packed houses first in the playhouse and then throughout the world. At the Salt Palace, downtown Salt Lake's convention center arena, a cast of 300 presented the story of Mormon and Moroni in performances attended by 40,000. Together Ralph and Mark examined every word of the script to decide on scriptures, interpretations, settings, and emphases. In 1976, Mark enjoyed the special bicentennial production of *Above All Other Lands*, which was adapted from his book *The Great Prologue*. The production, held in the Special Events Center at the University of Utah, attracted a total of 50,000 to several performances. *Behold the Lamb of God*, based on the Savior's visit to the American continent, highlighted the Easter season for those of all denominations who attended. The play was eventually seen by a million people throughout the world.

Mark's association with Elder David B. Haight during the Promised Valley years was one of love and esteem. The elder apostle liked to tell his associates how Elder Haight did all the work and gave Mark all the glory. Mark continued to supervise the Pageant Committee of the Church, constantly

upgrading the quality of the various productions and the visitors' centers, using a soft, effective approach to love people
into the Church.

Ralph Rodgers declared, "I know of no other person who
spent more of his life using the arts to bring people to the
gospel. I never ceased to learn from him. He was first and
foremost dedicated to the Church and lived his religion totally. I think that when history records in years to come the
good that has been done through great productions, through
visitors' centers, through drama, through pageants, and
through the arts, the name of Mark E. Petersen would have to
lead the list of those making a contribution."

When he received an assignment to supervise the missions in Australia, New Zealand, and the South Pacific, Mark
was released as president of the Deseret News Publishing
Company and from the board of the Newspaper Agency Corporation. He continued, however, to write the editorials for
the *Church News*. Although the record shows that Mark left
the paper officially on June 29, 1971, he never really left the
Deseret News, for he continued to speak at funerals of deceased staffers, to call on the sick, to perform marriages, to
write letters of congratulations and condolence, to deliver
Christmas gifts, and to counsel children. The *Deseret News*
and Mark were inseparable.

The newspaper initiated a program to honor excellence
in journalism, culminating in the annual Mark E. Petersen
Awards banquet. Mark appreciated the recognition, but he
marveled at the changes since he began at the *Deseret News*.
When he was a reporter, there was no front entrance to the
paper's offices; the staff had to cut through a barbershop and
an alley to go to work. Replacing typewriters with computer
equipment was a star-wars type improvement. The expansion of the staff amazed him.

When his granddaughter Sydney became editor-in-chief
of her high school newspaper, she had to answer to her
grandfather for the quality of her stories, the length of her
headlines, the proofreading, the makeup, and the overall

quality of the paper. When she won an All-American citation for her paper, her grandfather knew that she had earned it.

Two years later Sydney's sister, Drew, took over as editor of the high school paper. The Brigham Young University student paper was delivered to Mark's office, and as he had done with Sydney, he compared Drew's newspaper to the BYU publication. Both girls understood that it was pointless to object to their high school paper's being compared with a college sheet. Their grandfather expected quality publications, and Drew, too, won an All-American citation for her paper.

If 1971 was difficult for Mark because of his release from the *Deseret News,* it became nearly unbearable with the death of his dear friend Richard L. Evans. As he spoke at the funeral, he said, "On this as yet unbelievable occasion, no words at my command can give expression to the feelings of the heart. Richard's passing is still incomprehensible to me. My poor tongue is powerless to describe a friendship which can only be felt in the depths of the soul." He referred to the great brotherhood in the Council of the Twelve: "They move as one; they work as one. They feel as one." His voice broke as he described Elder Evans as "greatly talented, brilliant of mind, charming of personality, humble of heart. He never rested from his task."

When Mark learned that Elder Evans was ill and that what had seemed to be a minor illness would prove fatal, his emotions left him speechless. Elder Evans had traveled the world as international president of Rotary Club and had preached the gospel in all corners of the earth. His self-denial and total dedication to the truth had led him to this final illness with a body too exhausted to fight for recovery. The Sunday morning a week before his death, when Elder Evans became aware that it was time for the Tabernacle broadcast that he had carried on for so many years, although he was only semi-conscious he tried to leave his hospital bed to take over his responsibilities at the microphone. During the time of the broadcast he went into convulsions three times, so upset was he to miss the program. When the broadcast was concluded, he became peaceful again.

Hearing all this, Mark was heartbroken, inconsolable. His relationship with Richard Evans had been closer than with any other man. Both had grown up in homes blessed with poverty. As children, both had carried newspapers. Both had come under the influence of great men in the Church while very young. Both had a sense of adventure. Again quoting from Mark's funeral talk, "It is that adventurous spirit now which will be further satisfied as Richard explores the reaches of the world of immortality, a world of which he has spoken and written much, a world where wait his father and mother, old friends like Dr. John A. Widtsoe and Albert E. Bowen and Emma Lucy Gates [Elder Bowen's wife], Lester F. Hewlett, and Jessie Evans Smith, who will delight to show him about and introduce him to that near but distant land. What an experience it will be to stand in the presence of God! What an experience for this apostle to come home to the Lord Jesus Christ and hear the Savior say, 'Well done, thou good and faithful servant.'"

Mark's entire family was aware of the torture he suffered knowing of his best friend's mortality, being glad that his reward was assured but still wondering how he could survive without him. Mark's grandson, Mark, particularly sensitive to the agony he was feeling, wanted to be sure to attend the funeral in the Tabernacle. His own best friend was moving and leaving on a mission, so young Mark had worn a heavy coat and boots to help with the move before driving to the funeral. When he arrived at the Tabernacle, an usher refused to let him enter the building without a suit, so he stood outside listening to his grandfather's voice break, wanting to be near and to help in some small way, not knowing what to do. He heard Grandpa Mark conclude with these words: "To this great advocate of truth we now bid a loving farewell. His work is finished here, but will go on and on in another sphere, and so we say:

Come lay his books and papers by, he shall not need them more.
The ink shall dry upon his pen so softly close the door.
His tired head, his mind so bright, now dimmed like winter's sun,
Will find sweet rest in heaven tonight, the teacher's work is done.

But is his work now really done? Is rest what Richard sought?
Shall his inspired talents now be lost and come to naught?
On other shores he'll wake today. New pens his hand will take,
New microphones his voice will send to comfort hearts that ache.

His noble thoughts, his wide appeal, in paradise will blend
With those of prophets long since gone. His work will never end."

Young Mark stood in the cold, gray afternoon waiting for the Twelve to emerge on the east side of the Tabernacle to join the cortege. When he spotted his grandfather, he walked to him to put his arm around him and tell him that he had done well. His grandfather looked so disconsolate that Mark was shocked. Grandpa Mark was the center of the universe in many ways for his grandchildren. He was the one person who, no matter how busy, could be relied upon to stop and listen. He knew their hopes and dreams and aspirations before anyone else. He was the rock of their security. Now as the young man saw his grandfather so downcast, he wondered if Grandpa Mark would ever again be the same.

12

Emma's Death

"Anguish and sorrows have taken her"
(Jeremiah 49:24)

As Mark and Emma's travels resumed and they criss-crossed the world from South America to Europe and back again, Emma's vitality seemed to lessen. She had previously shown great delight in taking an active part in meetings and seminars, injecting laughter and tears, always bearing her witness of the truth. She enjoyed writing books that Mark edited, and felt that the youth of the Church must be educated in the scriptures. When she met people who told her that they had read her Bible and Book of Mormon stories and learned from them as they taught their children, her pleasure was apparent. Now Mark sensed that she cared little for events around her, and he found himself leaving her with Peggy's family more and more as he traveled.

An alert hairdresser had noticed a mole growing on the top of Emma's head. Dr. Lealand Clark, a dermatologist who had trained at the Mayo Clinic, carefully removed the growth and sent it to the laboratory. The Petersens were leaving town and had pressured him to do the surgery in his office posthaste. Dr. Clark told Emma she must stay home and see a plastic surgeon. The innocuous little mole was a melanoma, the fastest-growing cancer known. Emma Marr entered LDS Hospital, where the doctors decided to take skin from her hip, replacing an area of scalp the size of a salad plate. With her hair partially removed, she would wear a wig the rest of her life.

Emma's fondness for rich foods was born in England, where the servants in her home in Liverpool smothered ev-

Emma Marr

erything with butter except the sweets, which they covered
with sugar and cream. A cholesterol problem resulted in a
series of small strokes.

A complicating factor was her age. At the time of the
Petersens' wedding, men always married younger women.
However, Emma was older than Mark—no one knew how
much until after her death. She circumvented the difficulty of
her years by using her own birthday, September 13, and
Mark's birth year, 1900. All the legal documents and government forms, not to mention insurance policies, show September 13, 1900, in her firm hand. After she died and her
daughters discovered that their mother had been putting on
a brave front and was actually several years older than they
knew, a new respect and understanding resulted.

In writing about her childhood unhappiness in private
school in England, Emma had spoken of her feelings of inferiority, "which still trouble me." Those who knew her saw

a brilliant mind, a great musical talent, and a flair for words. As the strokes continued, no physical damage was apparent, but her insecurities mounted. The family doctor prescribed medication that would prevent more strokes. Her new pills brought back the old Emma Marr, and everyone relaxed. Again she began to drive her bright yellow 422 Oldsmobile, delighting in its power and speed.

On their return from England, Emma insisted that the family home at 851 Diestel Road be sold and a move made to a large apartment on Fifth Avenue. Mark did not object, for now he could walk to work. He left the apartment early each morning, going from Fifth Avenue to South Temple, then down South Temple to the office. In spite of her former problems, Emma seemed well, taking organ lessons on Temple Square, teaching a Sunday School class, occasionally traveling with Mark.

One day she realized that her medication was nearly gone, so she drove to the neighborhood pharmacy. A policeman had recently visited her husband to complain about her refusal to recognize the "One Way" sign on Second Avenue. He told Mark that she flew up the street like an apparition, going the wrong way in her bright yellow car. So this day she drove sedately, observing all traffic signs. At the drugstore, she was pleased to discover that her favorite pharmacist stood behind the counter. When she gave him the empty bottle, he said, "Sister Petersen, you're taking the same medication as an epileptic."

Whether Emma understood the definition of epilepsy is unknown. Her finishing-school education in England had provided her with no knowledge of physiology, and she relied upon her daughters to tell her the location of organs being removed from acquaintances or diseases afflicting the population. But the way the druggist said *epilepsy* convinced her that she shouldn't associate herself in any way with this condition. She never took another pill, and she grew progressively worse. Her husband was grateful that Ricks College had presented her with a distinguished service award

*Mark and
Emma Marr*

on May 9, 1973, before her condition prevented her from understanding that event.

Mark had never really been alone before in his life. Growing up with Mona, his twin, provided companionship until his mission. On his return, he had discovered Emma Marr and proposed a month later. This relationship, sometimes stormy but always stimulating, provided the center of his existence. At first he took Emma Marr to Peggy's house the day he left for conference, picking her up on Sunday night when he returned or Monday if the assignment were a distant one. But Emma didn't sleep at night and kept him up talking for hours and hours, while Mark needed eight hours of sleep to function at top speed. So he began giving her to Peggy on Thursdays and leaving her until Tuesday, with only two nights without his rest every week.

It was decided that Emma would be kept at home, which was no longer the apartment on Fifth Avenue. As her illness progressed, she had recalled the happy days on Diestel Road.

One day, noticing a for-sale sign on a home across the street from their old house, she called the number, inspected the property, and immediately wrote a check for the amount of the mortgage. So at 852 Diestel Road the Petersens again found themselves in the Bonneville Ward. Four women were hired to watch after Emma in shifts, taking her on weekends to Peggy.

As Mark traveled, his wife's absence removed much of the enjoyment of his work. Their fiftieth wedding anniversary was observed with a family dinner, but the occasion was subdued because of Emma's condition. When Peggy's family purchased a home without stairs and with room to spare, Mark brought Emma to live with her daughter because an out-of-town assignment called in South America. As Emma stood in the front hall surveying the still-unpacked boxes and furniture, with her head held high, she declared, "How the mighty have fallen!"

The next months might have proved very difficult had not a kind friend and psychiatrist visited weekly to give guidance and support. With every stroke, Emma's memory of recent events receded. The doctor spoke to her gently, asking questions about what she was thinking and the time period she was in. When she died, she believed that she was a thirteen-year-old in Liverpool, that Peggy's son was her own brother, Jack, and that they were surrounded by strangers.

Mark, who was still living on Diestel Road, came daily after he finished at the office. Later he told the family that sometimes he had stood on the front porch for ten minutes before he could gather courage to enter the house and see his beloved Emma Marr, who no longer recognized him.

After spending most of the fall in South America, he again went to Sao Paulo, Santiago, and Buenos Aires in February, returning the end of March. On April 15, 1975, a week after general conference, Emma Marr died at 2:15 P.M. at Peggy's home. Watching his beloved wife lose her sharp mental abilities had broken Mark's heart. Intellectually he knew that she was happier on the other side. Emotionally he was bereft. How he missed her! Part of him died with her.

In his journal Mark wrote: "The services were held today [April 18] at 12:00 noon at the Bonneville Ward. Most of the General Authorities were there. Elder Hinckley and Sister Spafford told of their experiences with us in the old First Ward. The following remarks were included in President Kimball's beautiful talk: 'I think of Emma Marr Petersen as being a wise virgin who carried her lamp always full of oil and was always listening for the call "the bridegroom cometh." '

"We cannot say that Emma's death is calamity or disaster or tragedy, for if we did, it would be saying that mortality was preferable to early entrance into the spirit world and to eventual salvation and exaltation. If mortality be a perfect state, then death would be a frustration, but the gospel teaches us that there is no tragedy in death; there is frustration and tragedy in sin, only sin. I am thinking what a joy there will be in the reunion of herself and her mother whom she adored. . . .

"There is purpose in all things. We cannot always see it. We can see only short distances, but the Lord sees from the beginning to the end. . . . Death is a great blessing. Think what the world would be were there no death. Of course we are never quite ready for the change. God controls our lives, unless we foolishly have shortened or terminated them. We can rely upon His wisdom and knowledge and understanding. I am convinced that the Lord has planned our destiny. We can shorten our lives, but I think we cannot lengthen them very much. . . ."

The overwhelming driving force in Emma's life was her testimony of the truthfulness of the gospel of Jesus Christ. She had written thirteen church-related books, many of which are still available, having gone into over twenty printings. She gave most of her book royalties to the missionary fund, believing that this work was the most important in the world. She bore her witness to anyone who would listen, large congregations or the delivery people who came to her home. Fearless in her defense of the truth, valiant in service, she already knew the Savior to whom she would report. She had given up her father for the Church; she would have done the same with her entire family, if necessary. She truly was a good and faithful servant of the Master.

One day after her death, while he was looking through her checkbook, Mark found the following: "Be strong and of a good courage; be not afraid, neither be thou dismayed; for the Lord thy God is with thee whithersoever thou goest." (Joshua 1:9.)

Emma Marr Petersen had the following goals: "I shall read a scripture daily and think of it during the day. I shall fill my mind with thoughts of charity, confidence, contentment, and courage. I shall strive always to cultivate and increase my talents, for my own self-respect as well as for the good of others. I shall try to improve my disposition and overcome any habits I have acquired of complaining, criticizing, faultfinding, nagging, and self-pity. I shall always have a project of some kind, wherein I shall work to serve others, or improve myself intellectually, spiritually, or socially."

13

Family and Friends

"O Lord, heal me; for my bones are vexed"
(Psalm 6:2)

Understanding the depth of Mark's sorrow, the First Presidency felt that a trip to South America to create and reorganize some stakes might help him adjust to his great loss. It was during these travels that he had an experience that brought him very close to the Lord. When he was twelve years old on a scout trip, he had been struck in the back by a boulder loosened by another hiker, and from that time he had gradually lost the feeling in his right leg and foot. In an age when back surgery was almost unheard of and rarely successful when performed, he bore the numbness without much thought. From time to time back pain troubled him, but it eventually went away, so he chose to ignore it.

In Brazil the pain struck him as never before. It was so excruciating that he was unable to lie down. All through every night he sat in a chair in his hotel room, praying for help and hoping the next morning might bring relief. He could not understand why he should suffer so while he was about the Lord's business, but the agony remained. A three-week trip stretched ahead of him. Finally he decided that the Lord wanted him in South America, for whenever he rose in a meeting to preach, the pain miraculously left him until he finished, and he enjoyed inspiration such as never before in his life. He felt sure that the Lord was sending him some sort of reassurance that Emma Marr was all right and that the Spirit remained with him to comfort him in his bereavement. Still the pain persisted, and for three weeks he was unable to lie down in bed. He left Buenos Aires early one morning to fly straight through to Salt Lake City. When he got off the plane, he noticed that it was difficult to move his right foot. However, just when he would have called the doctor, the Church sent him to speak at a special missionary fireside in the Seattle Coliseum. Then he conducted the Bellevue Washington Stake conference and toured the Seattle Washington Mission. Again the intense pain disappeared as soon as he rose to his feet to speak.

Mark was delighted that in his absence the First Presidency had reassigned him as supervisor of the missions in the British Isles, with Elder Bernard P. Brockbank as area supervisor. But he returned to Salt Lake City almost dragging his right leg, still wondering how he could possibly stand the pain. He somehow got home from the airport, crawled into bed—and the next morning discovered that he could not move. Painfully he dialed Peggy's number. She called his orthopedist, who immediately put him in the hospital. It was a cold summer, and the doctors commented that on July 2, the day a laminectomy was performed, the cars parked outside had a light covering of snow. Drs. Reed Fogg and Oliver Johnston working together performed a quick, accurate operation that relieved the problem. Mark was delighted to hear that his heart and lungs were those of a thirty-five-year-old.

Dr. James Webster, a cardiovascular specialist, was determined that all should go well after the operation. Following the laminectomy, he asked the nurses to call him hourly all night long and give him Mark's blood oxygen level. Mark had been placed in an older area of the hospital where oxygen was not piped into the room, so an oxygen tank stood next to his bed. All night long Dr. Webster waited for the blood oxygen level to rise. It never happened. The next morning he discovered the reason. Someone had changed tanks and failed to restart the machine. Dr. Webster became furious. He went to the nurses' station and asked all those on duty to come with him to Elder Petersen's room. There he lined them up at the bottom of Mark's bed and shouted, "Elder

Petersen, I want you to look at these people. They have been trying to kill you." With this, Dr. Webster unplugged the bed, wheeled Mark through the hospital, and put him into a room where he felt the care was superior.

A beautiful friendship had begun. Dr. Webster lived next door to Peggy and her family. He had introduced himself to Mark at this time and had discussed the gospel with him with great enthusiasm. He had visited Emma Marr and held long conversations with her. When a physician close to the Petersens and the Websters found himself in drug troubles, Jim Webster had called at Mark's office to discuss possible remedies. Always the conversation returned to the gospel. Now he attempted to control the clots that might put Mark in the category of having a successful operation in which the patient died. Needless to say, the hospital staff watched Mark's oxygen carefully. After two weeks he was released to Peggy's home.

Again Mark felt the power of the Spirit of the Lord. By August 26 he had returned to the office. The results of the surgery were miraculous, and he wasn't sure whether the skill of his fine physicians or the power of healing had cured him. Knowing that the doctors had fasted as they operated touched him deeply.

Following general conference, Mark was assigned to England. He flew to London with Peggy and her husband. They were to visit with their daughters, Sydney and Drew, who were spending a semester abroad with BYU in London, and Grandpa Mark had conferences to conduct. Spending two days with the family before he went to work, he was amused to discover that the girls could go anywhere on the underground and knew London better than he himself, although he had lived there three years. He and the Bartons spent several glorious days sightseeing and revisiting his favorite London haunts. In England he felt no pain in his back for the first time since he was twelve years old.

In London, Mark stayed at the Rembrandt Hotel, his favorite in the British capital. This hotel was within walking distance of Hyde Park Ward and the Church visitors' center, the reason for his original booking. The graciousness of the hotel staff, the high-ceilinged old-fashioned dining room, and the enormous bathrooms with tubs large enough to launch a ship pleased Mark, who ignored the gently aging condition of the furnishings. When Murdock Travel in Salt Lake City suggested that he might enjoy a newer, grander accommodation, he objected strenuously. He was a Rembrandt patron for life.

It was on this trip that Mark, or rather his granddaughter Sydney, made a very happy discovery. One of the objections to the Book of Mormon that he had heard ever since he was a missionary was the description of horses on the American continent. A high school teacher and later some college professors argued with Mark that if he knew anything at all, he should realize that horses appeared only when brought by the Spanish explorers. If anything proved that the Book of Mormon was false, it was this claim that horses had existed in America before Columbus. Mark's faith had been unshakable even as a child, and he wished he had knowledge enough to refute these arguments. He was certain that they were wrong, but he could not explain them away.

Across from Hyde Park Ward was the British Museum of Natural History, which exhibits the places of origin of all the animals in the world. Sydney was a museum buff like her grandfather, who had spent every preparation day of his time as mission president doing Bible research at the British Museum. Somehow he had missed this museum. When Sydney, knowing of her grandfather's preoccupation with the origin of horses, discovered a large display supporting the Book of Mormon, she could hardly wait to take him to see it. He wrote, "This display [on horses] was a part of a setup on evolution. For a long time we have been told that there were never any horses in America until the Spaniards. This large display announced that horses originated in North America and from there spread to South America and to other parts of the world. They did say that for some reason horses became extinct in America shortly before the Spaniards came, but there is archeological evidence that horses were here in ancient times and they were native to America." Mark thought it was worth the trip to England to see this additional proof of the modern scriptures. Without the help of the Lord, Joseph Smith had no way of knowing that horses came from a spot near Missouri, any more than did Mark's teachers in school.

On November 13 Mark traveled to Europe and joined Elder Charles A. Didier in creating a new stake in Paris. Assignments in England the following weekend necessitated his remaining in London, and another visit with his two favorite girls was enjoyed by all. The IRA had been busy with bombs at this time, and before one entered a restaurant or store, purses and packages were searched by guards. Any unattended parcel at any public place was reported and examined immediately. Sydney and Drew took their grandfather to a Gilbert and Sullivan play and were astonished to discover on their return that a bomb had exploded at the rear of the Rembrandt Hotel. Fortunately the damage was minimal.

Mark's frequent visits to Onslow Gardens, the hotel where the BYU students stayed, resulted in all sorts of adopted grandchildren. Surrounded by enthusiastic college students, he felt less lonely for Emma but thought how much she would have enjoyed seeing her granddaughters mature, both seeking degrees in the English that she had so loved, both winning scholarships, both writing up a storm.

When granddaughter Sydney graduated from Brigham Young University with a 3.93 average and *summa cum laude* on her diploma, Mark sat in the audience and took pride in being the "grandfather of." This family joke originated when Marian and Peggy began accomplishing in athletics and scholastically. Regardless of the effort involved, they were designated never by name, only as the "daughters of." It seemed to them that if they did well, it was because they were Mark Petersen's daughters, and if they made a mess of something, it was also because they were Mark Petersen's daughters. When the grandchildren reached the point when honors came their way, they became the "grandchildren of." Occasionally they complained to Mark, who listened sympathetically. Young Mark explained that when he visited his friends, their parents always said, "Hello, Mark. How's your grandfather?" They never asked how he was. The boy liked his grandfather well enough to tolerate this minor irritation. But when Sydney entered J. Reuben Clark Law School and was designated the Stephen L Richards Scholar on the basis of her LSAT score and scholastic average, some of her classmates assumed that the real reason was that she was the "granddaughter of." She had worked hard to accomplish this goal and felt that possibly someone should give her a little of the credit. When she told her grandfather that once again the "granddaughter of" was getting in her way, Grandpa Mark looked her in the eye and asked, "How would you like to be the *of?*"

Until this time, none of the family had considered that the occurrences that sometimes caused them unhappiness made their father and grandfather equally uncomfortable. Lack of privacy weighed heavily on Mark at times. Going out to dinner with his family sometimes turned into a circus, with people pointing or stopping at the table to shake hands, ask doctrinal questions, introduce their children, or discuss their church callings. He was always happy to greet people, but he could enjoy the luxury of a private conversation with children and grandchildren only when they were outside of Salt Lake City.

After the Second World War, when Volkswagens were first imported to the United States, L. H. Strong had invited Emma to drive one of the little bugs. The amazing maneuverability had fascinated her as she made U turns on the sidewalk at her host's suggestion. Purchase a Volkswagen she must, and she enjoyed driving Mark to the Church office and watching eyes pop. When Jessie Evans Smith, President Joseph Fielding Smith's wife, saw Emma tooling around in her little black car, she too wanted to drive one of the German wonders. Knowing no one at the Volkswagen dealership, she asked Emma to pick her up on the corner of South Temple and State Street outside the Eagle Gate Apartments, where she and President Smith lived. When Emma appeared at the appointed hour, a crowd of ten ladies stood expectantly on the curb. Sister Smith explained that when she had told her neighbors she was going for a ride in a Volkswagen, magically they had all appeared to see if she would fit. Public curiosity bothered Jessie Evans Smith and Emma Marr not at all. In fact, they seemed to revel in it. But to Mark's children and grandchildren, the spotlight glared uncomfortably.

Whenever any of the family, immediate or otherwise, wanted financial help either in attending college or serving a mission, Mark generously opened his wallet. He gladly sent nephews on missions, providing clothing, monthly expenses, and other necessities, thankful that they were worthy of a call. He felt strongly about the Church's mission fund, which was used to help elders and sisters who had no other financial support. He gave the income from many of his books to this fund, and often joked that the books he donated to the Church sold many more copies than the volumes he kept for himself.

When Sydney and Drew, both with English degrees, decided to go to law school, this seemed natural enough to Mark, who had raised his three grandchildren to think independently and value scholastic achievement. Literally, the glory of God was intelligence to him, and he thrilled to see the girls learn. He firmly believed that every woman should be prepared with a career so that if she did not marry or if she married and lost her husband, she could support herself and any children in a comfortable way. The J. Reuben Clark Law School at BYU, dedicated to producing fine ethical attorneys, seemed the only place for his granddaughters. Mark was grateful to the Church for naming the school after President Clark, whose lofty achievements in law and United States foreign policy always reflected his integrity.

On December 17, 1979, Mark performed the marriage of

Mark with his granddaughter Drew, left, and daughter Peggy,
viewing Christmas scene on Temple Square

his granddaughter Drew and Anthony Badger Quinn. Bride
and groom both attended J. Reuben Clark Law School but
had met in Washington, D.C., while Tony was clerking for a
law firm and Drew served with Senator Jake Garn. Tony's
mission to Denmark seemed a fitting requirement for joining the Petersen Danes. The reception at the Barton home
glowed with fires in the fireplaces and Christmas decora-
tions. Drew was a beautiful bride in a Mexican lace gown, but
the real star of the show was Grandpa Mark, who greeted the
guests at the front door wearing a bright red velvet smoking
jacket. Drew, who had married during her second year in
law school, received her J.D. on a Friday some eighteen
months later and had John Anthony Quinn, Mark's first great-
grandchild, the following Monday.

When Mark received an assignment to Great Britain to divide the Huddersfield Stake and create the new Leeds Stake,
tour the London Mission, then hold stake conference in
Southampton and Reading stakes, he thought that he would

invite Sydney to accompany him as a graduation present. She had just graduated from BYU. And as long as he was buying airplane tickets, he purchased one for Peggy as well. On November 9 the trio flew to London. Mark was famous for his refusal to check any luggage. In his early travels, too often a bag had been lost or a plane missed while he was waiting for luggage to be transferred. Sydney and Peggy realized that if they were to travel with him for two weeks, their wardrobes would be limited to whatever they could squeeze into an overnight bag.

With so many interviews connected with three stake conferences plus a mission tour, Mark had little time for his two travel companions. They were on their own. Sydney and Peggy went to all the places that they remembered with fondness from previous visits to London, and because neither knew when they might return, certain purchases were made. Mark was staying in a room at the Rembrandt, as were they. When he called to take them to meals, both women were ready to dash into the hall, preventing his discovery of the pile of packages that seemed to be growing in their room.

With the return flight not far off, they went to Lillywhites, a wonderful sporting goods store on Piccadilly Circus, and purchased six heavy nylon bags. Into these six bags they stuffed their accumulation of shopping. Never checking baggage was an unbreakable family rule. Thus, when Mark's fellow travelers appeared for the ride to the airport with six extra bags, he was speechless. At the airport, he helped them check their luggage, still without comment.

Sydney and Peggy would have preferred a rousing air-clearing lecture, until they noticed the amusement that Grandpa Mark tried so desperately to conceal. A security man was picking up another member of the Twelve at the Salt Lake Airport when they arrived, and to see Elder Petersen, who never carried luggage, struggling under six brightly colored bulging nylon bags was just too good a story not to pass along. Mark's fellow workers during the next few days gave him as bad a time as possible and never let him forget that he had flown home from England having checked not one but six bags.

Even before he moved permanently into Peggy's home, Mark liked to spend his spare time writing at her desk, then editing in the backyard with an Irish wolfhound at his feet. As he read a passage aloud and reworked phrasing, two large, intelligent eyes watched his face and hung on every word. His grandson wondered if anyone would buy his books if it became known that they had first been read to a dog. Mark enjoyed working at this house where Emma Marr had died, but bittersweet memories sometimes intruded on his thoughts. Diestel Road seemed increasingly empty to him. Even when the family was away, the Barton dogs delighted in his visits.

Mark had first seen Irish wolfhounds when he lived in Great Britain. In Ireland the natives talked of the difficulties of keeping a 150-pound dog during the food shortages of World War II and of families so devoted to the breed that they moved with their canines near United States bases in Britain so they could feed them camp leftovers. Irish wolfhounds do not bite, but they place their full weight upon the enemy until their masters arrive. When Granddaughter Drew spent hours cross-stitching this quotation from early Britain, Mark proudly hung it on his wall: "I will give thee a dog which I got in Ireland. He is huge of limb and for a follower equal to an able man. Moreover he hath a man's wit and will bark at thine enemies but never at thy friends. He will see by a man's face whether he be ill or well-disposed towards thee. He will lay down his life for thee."

When Mark was assigned to organize a new stake at Aarhus, Denmark, his brother Claude accompanied him at his own expense and looked forward to practicing his Danish on the natives. As a boy in Salt Lake City, Claude had served as interpreter to their Danish grandparents when they went to the store or had business to conduct downtown. He was certain that with his wide knowledge of the language, he would please and surprise all whom they met. But the

Dave Newman Photography

Back, left to right: Mark's sister Phoebe, Mark, and Mona (Mark's twin).
Front: Mark's brother Claude and Claude's wife, Thelma

Danish that Claude had spoken seventy years previous
seemed to bear no relationship to the Danish currently spoken in Denmark. The Danes could not understand Claude
and Claude could not understand the Danes, much to Mark's
amusement.

Claude and Mark visited Hvorup, where their mother
was born. They found the church in which she was christened and confirmed a member of the Lutheran faith. A visit
to Aalborg produced a reunion with three cousins whose
family the Petersens had sponsored to come to the United
States.

Following Emma Marr's death, Claude and his wife,
Thelma, often came to Salt Lake City from California to spend
the summer with Mark. Thelma had been a nurse in charge
of the recovery room at Primary Children's Medical Center,
and her unbending devotion to good principles of health occasionally drove Mark to Peggy's house for a square meal.
Thelma was a formidable enemy of malnutrition, overweight,
and overwork. But loving, well-meaning, kind, and gentle, she

inflicted no rules she was not willing to accept herself. Mark look forward to these visits, enjoying the companionship of a family again. When Thelma had a fatal coronary, Mark felt saddened. He was especially touched by S. Dilworth Young's poem about her. It begins, "Who can measure the soul of Thelma Petersen? Her heart reached out to touch the aged and the poor, and children small. And in her life she gave them more, gave all she could of service."

Of those people indispensable to Mark, Dorene Wagstaff, his secretary, ranked near the top. Dorene seemed to know instinctively what to do in large and small emergencies, and she ran the office with tact and aplomb. While Mark traveled, she quietly kept things moving, recognizing the problems that needed delegation and those that could wait for his return. Confidential matters were safe with her, and Mark enjoyed her friendship as well as the working association. When he heard that she had met someone she considered marrying, Mark's first reaction was that no one could be good enough for Dorene. Then came the realization that he couldn't possibly work without her. Charles James Beagles was a convert to the Church of two years. Formerly a New York broker, he had left New York and gone to France, where the missionaries found him. After his baptism, Charles, a native Oklahoman, felt strongly that he should go to Salt Lake City. Arriving in Zion, he went to church on Sunday, saw Dorene, and knew why he had come.

On the morning of August 15, 1980, Mark, Dorene, Charles, family members, and friends went through an early session of the Salt Lake Temple. Then, in a nearby sealing room, Mark united Dorene and Charles Beagles for time and all eternity. Once their decision to become man and wife had been made, Mark became as excited as anyone else and insisted on hosting a wedding breakfast at the Lion House for the happy couple.

After Emma Marr's death, Mark found that he would rather be on the road for the Church than alone at his home on Diestel Road. He enjoyed touring missions and occasion-

ally stayed during the week between conferences with some
of the First Quorum of the Seventy who were living in the
field. His visit with Elder Loren Dunn in Sydney, Australia,
was particularly pleasant. Elder Dunn, the son of a printing
family from Tooele, Utah, led his mission with authority and
skill. The Dunn children welcomed their visitor and treated
him as a grandparent. Mark's pleasure at watching the gospel
work in their home was apparent. Similar experiences with
the Gene Cook and Grant Bangerter families followed.

But Mark couldn't travel all the time. When he was home,
Although Mark's own scouting career had ended at the
tenderfoot level, he enjoyed his work on the Boy Scouts of
America council and was particularly impressed by his experience in Colorado Springs at the National Jamboree. At a
Region 12 meeting of the organization, he was presented
with the Silver Antelope Award. He took special pleasure in
the two persons involved—Elder Delbert L. Stapley, a close
associate in the Twelve, made the presentation, and Elder
Marion D. Hanks of the First Quorum of the Seventy read the
citation.

But Mark couldn't travel all the time. When he was home,
the emptiness of the house always surprised and depressed
him. His typewriter seemed his best friend, and if he couldn't
sleep, he wrote. The bishopric of the Bonneville Ward visited
often, bringing gifts of food and giving home teaching lessons. The theater organ in the living room was a constant re-
minder to Mark of the evenings he and Emma had spent
singing together. The Royal Copenhagen bears, the jade ele-
phants, the carved ivory tower—wherever he looked he saw
souvenirs of trips they had taken together. Loneliness seemed
a constant companion.

If any of Mark's personal characteristics had irritated
Emma Marr, it was his insistence on promptness. "Living
with deadlines for forty years has left its Mark," she used to
declare as she arrived on the arm of her husband at airports,
parties, meetings, and various other appointments at what
seemed to her hours before anyone else. Mark like to quote
President Heber J. Grant, who said, "I have wasted more time

Top: Mark shows Silver Antelope award to Elder Delbert L. Stapley.
Bottom: Mark greets Scouts at National Jamboree in Colorado Springs

being on time waiting for others than in any other way." This also exasperated Emma, who thought that if Mark realized that being early was a waste of time, he should cease and desist. He never replied to her complaints, just made sure they arrived even earlier the next time.

When Mark was invited to join President Spencer W. Kimball's party for area conferences in England, he traveled to Great Britain ten days early to reorganize the Hull Stake, divide Sunderland Stake, visit the Birmingham Mission, and prepare for the creation of the new Preston Stake. With the Kimball group he visited the River Ribble, where the first baptisms in England were performed by Heber C. Kimball in 1837. Eight thousand Saints attended one of the meetings in England and heard President Kimball speak for an hour about his relationship to Heber C. Kimball and some of the early missionary experiences in the Preston area.

An immediate friendship had developed between Camilla Kimball and Emma Marr when their husbands became members of the Twelve. Both women loved learning and read voraciously. As the Kimballs and Petersens traveled together, the wives enjoyed meeting the people, seeing the sights, sharing personal glimpses of their families, and bearing testimony of the truth. Now Emma Marr was absent for the first time, and as Mark watched Spencer and Camilla together, he ached for his own dear companion. The pain of his loss seemed almost overwhelming. Everywhere he saw families together, husbands and wives at each others' sides. Now only he was alone. In his room he struggled with his emotions, realizing that he must join the group, wishing he could hide. Suddenly he became aware of a comforting feeling, and he knew without a shadow of a doubt that at that very minute when he felt so bereft, Emma Marr was praying for him. Realizing that he could never be alone, that his dear Emma understood his sadness and stood by his side, he felt at peace. From that time his acceptance of her death was complete.

One day as Peggy sat in her father's office waiting to go to lunch with him, she looked at the photograph of Richard L. Evans that Mark kept near his desk and wondered aloud what Elder Evans was doing at the moment. Mark, who was finishing an article for the *Ensign* and obviously concentrating on his typewriter and not the conversation, replied, "Oh, I don't know. He's probably talking with your mother."

Serving as chairman of the Leadership Training Executive Committee, which was responsible for training Regional Representatives, stake presidents, and bishops, was one of Mark's favorite assignments. His skill at the chalkboard and his conviction that the Church should be made more aware of the sanctity of the ordinances of baptism and sacrament gave him an enthusiasm for the assignment. He always preached that the sacrament and baptism were the two most sacred ordinances performed outside the temple. Realizing that the sacrament was a special time, he hoped that the Saints would truly remember their Savior and his suffering for them. When from the stand he observed casual partaking of the bread and water, he felt sure that ignorance prompted the action.

Mark had borne strong testimony of the Savior even as a missionary. But as he grew in the gospel and served so many years as a special witness, those close to him noticed that his sermons on the Christ had a slightly different quality. No longer were there any "I believes." He began to speak as if he had received some personal manifestation. As he referred to Jesus with such solemn knowledge, his family wondered if he had seen the Christ, but being well-brought-up by an excellent father and grandfather, they knew better than to ask. Mark always taught those close to him that certain things were too sacred to be discussed.

14

Love for His Fellowman

"Faith in his name hath made this man strong"
(Acts 3:16)

From the first time Mark heard the song "Dare to Be a Mormon," he had dared to do many things. If he felt something was right, he did not hesitate to try to accomplish the means to make the changes necessary. Now he seemed to appoint himself a doctrinal watchdog, and if anything was printed that he knew was incorrect, he wrote to the people involved. When he read an article in the *Ensign* that presented a false teaching as to how the Bible passages quoted in the Book of Mormon came about, he sent off a five-page letter to the magazine advisers listing the reasons that the disputed theory should be discarded. He wrote, "I was greatly disappointed that the author would perpetuate this unfortunate theory. . . . I attach a Xerox copy and have marked the paragraphs which I hope may be forgotten and never used again."

If Mark was aware that any of the General Authorities or Regional Representatives might be preaching doctrine not in harmony with Church teachings, he never hesitated to point out the error in their thinking. How he wished that everyone would stay close to the Prophet! Only through the President of the Church could new doctrine be introduced. When questionable books were delivered to his office, he often gave them to Dorene with the comment, "Take this and read it, but don't believe it."

Mark loved people. He loved those around him. If he has been judged by the way he judged others, his reward is great. Over and over in his sermons he reiterated his belief that the

results of one's life boil down to this issue: How did one respect other people? Regardless of the amount of church con-
tributions, the number of meetings attended, the high positions held, if a person failed to treat others honestly and well,
if he showed no charity for his brothers, if kindness was lack-
ing, all else would be forgotten.

Years before, soon after he was called to the Twelve,
Mark went to a stake conference to change a presidency and
found that the first counselor had his heart set on leading the
stake. Inspiration told Mark to choose another man. The first
counselor, disappointed and bitter, took his wife and family
and joined a different denomination in the community. His
children, young at the time, grew up in another religion. The
values and precepts so important to the man and his wife
never reached them. All of the family paid for the action of
their father. Mark began to write letters to this man as soon as
he heard that he had left the Church, trying to show him the
error of his ways. He continued the correspondence until
the time of his death. He never criticized or accused. He truly
loved this brother.

As he traveled the world, it was exciting for Mark to teach
of the Savior and to see eyes light up at the thought of the
scope of the Lord's mission. When he heard the number of
baptisms that followed his talks, he exulted that so many
were touched by the Spirit. As more and more people asked
for healing blessings, and word reached him of the lame
who walked and the blind who saw, he remembered the
promise in the blessing he had been given by Elder Nicholas
G. Smith, and he was humbled.

When Mark was assigned to talk to the student body of
Brigham Young University, he decided to address the subject
of "Christ the Creator," combining his two favorite subjects,
religion and astronomy. He had a sure testimony that Christ
was the literal Creator and that the Book of Genesis con-
tained the most accurate description of the creation of the
world available to mankind. As he realized the immensity of
the universe and the comparatively inconsequential place of

*Mark E. Petersen
at a general
conference session
shortly after
Emma Marr's death*

earth's solar system, Mark was thrilled to contemplate the innumerable worlds created by our Elder Brother. When Christ came to earth as a little babe in Bethlehem, born to the lowliest of families, He was still the great Jehovah, Lord of heaven and earth.

Feeling that a suitable time had elapsed since Emma Marr's death, President N. Eldon Tanner called Mark into his office one day to inform him of the First Presidency's wish that he remarry. From the time of Emma's funeral, Mark had received countless proposals from women who were sure that they could brighten his life. Dorene, his secretary, always faithful and willing to do anything to make her boss's life simpler, read many of these letters and filed them carefully away. Similar mail arrived at Mark's home address, where he disposed of it. The truth was that Mark felt that during Emma's illness he had not been able to give to the Church the total dedication that was now possible. With no one waiting at home, he could work through the evening when necessary. Lengthy traveling assignments caused no problem. For the first time in years, he could live totally for the Lord. He had collected fourteen different Bible translations, and he wanted to go through each carefully. His library held many books with illuminating quotations from scientists attesting to their belief in a divine creation. He especially liked Albert Einstein's statement: "The harmony of natural law reveals an Intelligence of such superiority that compared to it, all the scientific thinking and acting of human beings is an utterly insignificant reflection." Dr. Oscar Leo Brauer, physicist, agreed. He stated: "Science can establish that a creative act at some time must have taken place, implying the existence of a Divine Power. Science can also establish that none but a Divine Intelligence could have been the author of the tremendously involved and intricate system of laws in the universe." And Mark loved this statement from Lord Kelvin, widely respected British scholar: "If you think strongly enough, you will be forced by science to believe in God."

Mark wanted to put all this together for the youth of the Church. Why should they struggle over the basic concepts that scientists and religionists have discussed for years, when facts support religion? If he were married, there just wouldn't be time to do justice to his work, let alone a wife. After a brief consultation, the First Presidency gave him permission to stay single.

A crusade began with Mark laboring at top speed. He was delighted to discover the Modern American Translation by Smith and Goodspeed, which read as follows: "In the beginning was the Word, and the Word was with God, and the Word was Divine. Everything came into existence through Him, and apart from Him nothing came to be. It was by Him that life came into existence." Mark considered these declarations amazing. Repeatedly he told audiences, "Jesus Christ, our Redeemer and Savior, created all things under the direction of His Father, including life, and He did so according to a preconceived plan. He was the Creator of heaven and earth. This is the position that we Latter-day Saints must take with respect to the Lord Jesus Christ. If we truly believe in Him, we must believe His doctrine, and this is the doctrine of

Christ. Are we willing to believe it? Are we willing to be Christians within the framework of this definition?" Then, as a special witness of the Savior, he would bear his testimony as to the truth of these facts.

Mark became convinced that until the Latter-day Saints read the scriptures for themselves, their testimonies rested on the beliefs of others. He devised a plan that he introduced at all his stake conferences. He asked his listeners to raise their hands if they would be willing to read the four Gospels. Then he pointed out that by reading a chapter of the Bible every day, very soon they could complete the New Testament. As he told them, "Take His yoke upon you and *learn* of Him," his voice swept his audience along with enthusiasm.

When members seemed to lag in support of the full-time missionaries living within their neighborhoods, Mark would call the elders to the stand at stake conference, one ward at a time, introduce them, and ask all those living in their ward to rise. Smiling and enjoying himself greatly, he would tell the people to take a careful look at the missionaries, because they would be calling soon at their homes. Then, raising his own hand, he always asked, "How many of you good people will invite your friends who have not joined the Church to come for a social evening and meet the elders?" Every hand would shoot up.

It has been said that a person who is liked by dogs and kids cannot be all bad. When they were on church assignments, the Twelve often stayed at members' homes. Mark enjoyed these visits, particularly if there were children. He felt most comfortable on the floor with a toddler, or poring over a game board with an older child. When he was driven to the airport, youngsters often asked what relation he was to them, not understanding that a person taking so much interest was not a family member.

Pets were always important to the Petersens, and a variety of animals lived with them. Emma Marr adored dogs, and the dogs loved her. As her illness progressed, she may have forgotten the names of family members, but she always recalled

the names of the dogs. Tory, an Irish wolfhound, sat end-
lessly with Emma, regarding her with soft brown eyes, seem-
ing to sense her distress. Mark too loved dogs, and when
Tory died of old age, he purchased another Irish wolfhound,
Bryn. Bryn knew her master and recognized the sound of his
car. According to folklore, an Irish wolfhound can tell by a
stranger's countenance whether he wishes his master good
or ill. Mark always enjoyed seeing visitors' reactions to his
hairy beast. One day when Elders Thomas S. Monson and
Bruce R. McConkie came to Mark's home for a meeting, Bryn
made a beeline for Elder McConkie. Elder Monson, delighted, commented, "Bruce, at last you have found someone
large enough to intimidate you." Mark enjoyed repeating this
episode, chuckling each time he thought of a 150-pound dog
trying to climb into Elder McConkie's lap.

Mark's kindness to others occasionally placed him in unusual circumstances. When Sarah McDonald had joined the
Church in Liverpool, a close friend, Carrie Macnamara, also
was baptized. Carrie came from a staunch Catholic family
who immediately disowned her. But, convinced of the truth
of the Church, she realized that even if her earthly family had
rejected her, a kind Heavenly Father extended all the love
she could need.

Carrie and Sarah continued to correspond after Sarah left
England to go to Canada. When Carrie heard that the
McDonalds had moved to Zion, she also traveled to Utah.
Eventually she became a recluse, and rather than resume her
career as schoolteacher, she chose to live on church and
state welfare. While she kept her person immaculately clean,
her clothing came from kind friends, the Deseret Industries,
and eventually downtown trash barrels. She lived in a shanty
and paid little rent. Carrie's uniform consisted of crepe-soled
men's shoes, a long black dress, several sweaters, a coat in
cold weather, and an elegant black hat. Every day she made
her way to the Salt Lake Public Library, where she spent many
happy hours stretching her brilliant mind.

If Mark encountered Carrie on the street, he always

stopped to talk. When his children accompanied him, they knew the wrath of their father would descend if they seemed self-conscious about greeting this oddly dressed woman or said anything that might embarrass her. Emma and Sarah had always referred to her as "Carrie Poor Soul." Peggy still remembers with embarrassment her attempt to introduce Carrie to a school friend at the library one day. When she returned home, she was chagrined to learn that Carrie's last name was Macnamara and not Poorsoul, as she had introduced her.

As the years passed, Carrie continued to forage in trash cans for food and clothing or any item that might be saleable, while her welfare checks piled up. Every day she went about her rounds downtown, visiting financial institutions, depositing her welfare checks, clutching a fistful of bank books in her hand, then going to the library to read.

One Christmas morning, the phone rang at Peggy's house. A Catholic priest called with the news that Carrie Poor Soul had died. Typically, she had listed Mark Petersen as next of kin. Mark was in England, so his daughters found themselves planning a funeral and buying a casket. The chapel at the mortuary was filled to capacity for the funeral. When Peggy and Marian had expressed their concern that there would be few mourners, the funeral director had replied that some retired people in the community had nothing to do but attend funerals. Happily, they all seemed to have come to send Carrie Pool Soul to her Maker.

During the time Mark was working on the two newspapers in Cincinnati, he had attended church every Sunday in the same ward and noticed a black family sitting on the back bench of the chapel. Mark always took note of anyone who seemed to be alone and made it a point to introduce himself. Every Sunday he greeted this family, admiring their beautiful children, who sat so reverently through the services. Later the family, unhappy with some of the racial problems they encountered in Cincinnati, decided to move to Utah. When they arrived in Salt Lake City, they contacted Mark. Just as the

Petersen daughters learned a great lesson of tolerance and love with Carrie Pool Soul, so with the Hope family they were shown how to interact with people of other races. At that time Salt Lake City had very few nonwhite citizens. By his actions, Mark demonstrated to his daughters that each person in the world is a child of God. As he visited this little family in their humble home, he often included his daughters.

Another person whom he befriended was Albert L. Zobell, Jr., a brilliant writer and historian. When he spoke at Albert's funeral, Mark described him as a man who had risen above some very severe physical difficulties and almost lifelong paralysis, graduating with highest honors from the University of Utah. Albert had written many books and more than 125 articles for the Church magazines, and was one of the top researchers in the Church. What Mark did not say was that before Albert had accomplished all of these things, he had been so overwhelmed by his disabilities that he had had little hope for the future. It was Mark's encouragement and faith in him that put him on the road to achievement.

Mark had a wonderful sense of humor. He especially enjoyed puns and an obvious play on words. He frequently found humor to lighten solemn occasions. He recalled with great relish a banquet he and Emma attended at the Hotel Utah with President Ernest L. Wilkinson of BYU and Sister Wilkinson. The wives hung their fur coats side by side as they proceeded into the dining room. When a huge slice of roast prime rib was served to each guest, Emma immediately thought of the family dogs waiting at home. Carefully she slipped part of her meat into a plastic bag in her evening purse and, excusing herself, went to place the bag in the pocket of her fur coat. It was only when she returned home and discovered that the meat was not in her coat that she realized she had hidden the doggy tidbit in Sister Wilkinson's coat and not her own. Mark thought this marvelously funny and could not wait until he saw President Wilkinson again to find out where the beef was.

When Mark was first called to the Twelve, he often had to travel to stake conferences in the southern end of Utah. On one occasion when he had been in Sanpete County, he was extremely tired and distracted as he drove toward home. As he followed a long line of cars on the two-lane road, a flashing red light suddenly interrupted his reverie. Mark felt that this was the last straw—he had not been exceeding the speed limit. He had wondered why the lead car continued to lag, but as he tried to explain this to the highway patrolman, the icy gaze met his and convinced him that he might as well accept the ticket.

At home that evening, when he emptied his pockets, he discovered the traffic violation and saw to his surprise that it was made out to D. K. Brown. Puzzled, he examined his license and noted under hair color, "dk. brown." He sent the ticket and a letter to the judge listed on the form and explained that his name was Petersen, not Brown. He did not receive a reply, but for years, when he was asked to write his name, he always queried, "Do you want M. E. Petersen or D. K. Brown?"

When Mark received a letter informing him that he had been selected for an Emeritus Club Merit of Honor Award at the University of Utah, he had mixed emotions. Though happy about his selection, he was somewhat offended at being included in this illustrious, yet elderly group. He did not consider himself old. He continued to drive himself to work, staying longer than many of his younger colleagues. He swam almost daily at the Deseret Gym and proudly maintained his pre-mission weight. Whenever anyone reminded him of the three beds he broke on his mission, he replied that in Canada he was taking care of weightier things. If he returned from a conference or a mission tour a few pounds heavy, he lived on cottage cheese until the scales returned to 180. He disciplined himself both in diet and exercise, attempting in this way to honor the Word of Wisdom. "Moderation in all things" did not include extremes in eating.

With his vigorous schedule, one might think Mark would want to slow down and rest occasionally, but he continued to chair many key church committees. In his spare time he enjoyed carpentry, house painting, and writing books. He kept in close contact with his granddaughters, Sydney and Drew, when they were both attending the J. Reuben Clark Law School at BYU. Thinking of all the rent money that could be saved, he purchased a duplex near the campus and became the girls' landlord, dealing with wallpaper and sprinkling systems and the tenant on the other side who regularly smuggled an unhousebroken puppy into her bedroom.

Mark was in Quito, Ecuador, at the home of President and Sister Gene Cook when he received a phone call from President Kimball asking for his approval in extending the priesthood to all worthy male members. Francis M. Gibbons, secretary to the First Presidency, read to Mark the statement that was to be published concerning the revelation.

Mark recalled, "I was delighted to know that a new revelation had come from the Lord. I felt the fact of the revelation's coming was more striking than the decision itself. On the telephone I told President Kimball that I fully sustained both the revelation and him one hundred percent." Mark's first reaction was to think of the joy in the black family whom he had befriended in Cincinnati. Never dreaming that he would ever hold the priesthood until the hereafter, Brother Hope still lived the life of a true Latter-day Saint.

Although driven by an insatiable thirst for knowledge, Mark loved every minute of his life. The excitement he felt never lessened as he pored over his fourteen Bibles, devoured the Book of Mormon, studied the sciences, peered through his telescope, and planned new ways to educate both leaders and members of the church. He was perhaps at his best in front of an audience of missionaries and investigators, explaining the signs of the true church, or speaking to the youth of new discoveries in the heavens. Describing the vastness of the works of Christ the Creator, he would draw pictures in the air of the infinity of space and the tiny place in a far corner where earth's insignificant solar system lay almost hidden away. His enthusiasm was electric, and those sitting on the stand would be fascinated by the seemingly mesmerized audience before them. Or was he at his best recalling the steps of the Master and His infinite sacrifice for man? His ringing testimony was unforgettable and often moved his listeners to tears.

He continued to travel to stakes every weekend, and his conference talks usually involved the audience, who were kept on the edges of their seats wondering what he would do next. Because he obviously enjoyed the people, they responded with love. When he found himself in a stake with a low percentage of tithe payers, his reaction was to work out a program of instruction to teach the members of the value of tithing. Education was his answer to most problems, and his teaching worked.

On an assignment to a special women's meeting in Los Angeles, Mark spoke two nights in a row with a total attendance of between 8,500 and 9,000 on the grounds of the Los Angeles Temple. One of his favorite subjects, the proper and important place for women in the Church and in the world, led him through his enthusiastic discourses. Mrs. Cathy Wright, honorary mayor of Simi Valley, was present on one of the evenings and afterward told her husband that it was one of the most amazing talks she had every heard. The ninety-year-old woman said, "I can't believe there are people who think the way I do about women."

The statues on women, the Relief Society's addition to the Los Angeles Temple grounds, attracted many who might not otherwise have come. Mark's beliefs that education and training for women are necessary, that regardless of future plans a woman must be taught to think, that marriage is not available to all, that the glory of God is intelligence, and that education is a part of religion, all made for interesting food for thought. When Mark's granddaughters chose to become attorneys, he rejoiced in their ambitions, then put them through law school, knowing that if their circumstances re-

Marian Petersen

quired them to support themselves, they would be trained and able. His daughter Marian's doctorate in music theory was also a source of great pride and pleasure.

During the 1981 Christmas vacation Grandpa Mark was delighted to observe that his granddaughter Sydney and Robert Bennion, a great-grandson of President J. Reuben Clark, seemed to have noticed each other for the first time, though Bob had been a close friend of grandson Mark for many years. Spontaneously the romance began to develop. The couple were married by Mark Petersen in the Salt Lake Temple the following May. Mark noted in his journal, "The reception at the Colonial House was very beautiful with lots of red roses and lily of the valley, and Syd looked glamorous in her wedding dress. All the men wore old-fashioned cutaway suits, which prompted merry comments from the brethren regarding my appearance. Syd and Bob will live in Los Angeles while Bob continues his medical training. Syd has been hired by the law firm of Morrison and Foerster and hopes to pass the California Bar in July."

Because his weekly assignments usually involved being away three of the seven days, and mission tours and overseas assignments lasted two or three weeks, Mark's responsibilities of home ownership now seemed overwhelming. With the granddaughters married, there was plenty of room in Peggy's home for him to have his own bedroom, study, and bath. He had spent more and more time at the Barton residence, and the thought of not returning to a cold, empty house appealed tremendously. Meanwhile, with clear weather, he planned to make good use of his telescope and read all the information he had assembled on Voyager One and the planet Saturn. He studied and wrote two editorials for the *Church News* titled "Lessons from Space" and "Interplanetary Talk." During his writing career, Mark had received various honors and accolades, but a note from Dr. James C. Fletcher, former president of the University of Utah and now head of NASA, pleased him enormously. It read: "The enclosed two articles from the *Church News* page are outstanding. They both show modern understanding of astrophysics and the nation's space program."

"Lessons from Space" discussed the complete regularity of the heavenly bodies in their movements, the precision that is everywhere present in the skies. In it Mark asked, Did this precision arise with a mighty accident or from the "Big Bang" theory of creation? Pointing out that explosions never bring order out of chaos, he stated that the heavens are well managed. He backed up his case with a quotation from Professor Conklin of Princeton University, who wrote, "The probability of life originating from accident is comparable to the probability of the unabridged dictionary resulting from an explosion in a printing factory." Mark's final paragraph concluded, "And who is the Creator and Manager of the heavens? Almighty God! Jesus Christ! 'All things were made by him, and without him was not anything made that was made' (John 1:3)."

"Interplanetary Talk" described the attempts of the United States and Russia to communicate with living beings on other planets. "But is there life out there?" Mark asked.

"Latter-day Saints know there is. According to Paul there are orbs that are telestial, terrestrial, and celestial. The Scriptures say that Jesus is the only Begotten of the Father, and that by Him and through Him and of Him the worlds are and were created." Mark's self-consciousness at not having a bachelor's degree made Dr. Fletcher's comment particularly welcome.

For the Jordan River Temple dedication, Mark was invited to speak for an hour at the first session. His memory for scriptures impressed his listeners, as did his forceful delivery when he bore witness to the necessity of work for the dead. His testimony of the Savior brought tears to many eyes. For the first time since his mission, when Sister Shaw had told him that she had seen a light while he spoke, several persons in the audience at the temple came to him after his talk and commented on the light that seemed to radiate from his face as he spoke. He minimized their comments until he was alone with his family, when he bore testimony to the strength of the Spirit he had felt.

While President Benson was recuperating from surgery for a hip transplant, Mark conducted meetings of the Twelve. He appreciated a note from Elder LeGrand Richards, commenting on his work: "You don't need to worry about the support of the members of the Quorum during President Benson's absence. They all love you very much, and you conduct the meetings with precision so that you get done what you have on your agenda to accomplish. Personally my love for you is very sincere. You don't only go the second mile, but you keep going in your kindness to me, looking after me in my old age, and I love you very much and appreciate your love and friendship more than you know. So, as long as I live, whatever your assignments and responsibilities are, you can count on me being back of you an hundred percent."

Because Mark and Elder Richards sat next to each other in Quorum meeting, they shared an occasional humorous aside. The younger apostle called for the grand old man of the Twelve at his home for quarterly Sunday meeting in the temple, and often helped him back and forth to weekday appointments as well. Elder Richards delighted in comparing Mark's kindness to that of a mother for a young child. The fact that Elder Richards was well into his nineties never entered the conversation.

Mark's move to his daughter's house would have been impossible without the kindness of Cottonwood 14th Ward members, especially Bishop and Sister Oliver Johnston and Elder Hugh Pinnock. Worldly goods did not burden Mark unless one counted his books. Elder Pinnock, his children, and his Volkswagen truck made repeated trips between the old and new residences with the truckbed filled with prized books. In earlier years Mark had been able to look at his bookcases at 851 Diestel Road and tell the name of any volume missing from any gap on any shelf. And if one of his family had made the mistake of loaning a book to a neighbor or friend, woe unto the perpetrator of the crime! That he allowed Elder Pinnock even to look at his library, let alone carry the volumes unescorted in his truck, showed the high regard in which Mark held this associate and neighbor.

Eagerly Mark looked forward to his first trip to Lake Powell. Always the student, he tried to learn everything about his surroundings. He had heard of the vastness of this man-made wonder and wanted to inspect it firsthand. Fortunately, Ed and Ann Bunting, who lived directly across the street, owned just the boat for such a trip. Ed managed to borrow a trailer with sleeping accommodations so that Mark need not spend nights on the boat. The thought of being out of uniform for a few days seemed too good to be true to Mark, who daily wore a white shirt and tie. At the lake, while Ed loaded the boat with food, Mark stood on shore in his bathing suit, a baggy shirt, sneakers, dark glasses, and a baseball cap, reveling in his freedom—the hot weather, no meetings, no white shirt, anonymity at last! As he savored these pleasures, a man walked toward him and said, "Hello, Elder Petersen." Mark complained, "How in the world did he recognize me in this getup?"

When they climbed to Rainbow Bridge and listened to

the ranger's explanation of its origin, a family of hikers joined
the group. After the talk and the questions from the tourists
concluded, the mother of the family approached Ann Bunting
to say that they had recently been converted to the Church in
New York. They had never been west, but, wanting to inspect
LDS headquarters, they had traveled to Salt Lake City and surroundings on their vacation. They were amazed that the first
General Authority they saw in the flesh would be an apostle
at Lake Powell.

Mark was a true Christian, one who humbly avoided recognition and honors for himself and was always concerned
about others. After his death, his family heard many things
about him that they had not before known. His motto, dis-
played in a frame on his desk at the office, was "No time to
lose," and for nearly eighty-four years he had driven himself
to learn, to work, to accomplish. But through it all, he took
the time to visit the sick and help the needy. When his next-
door neighbor on Diestel Road was placed in a nursing
home, Mark never failed to visit him. When one of his *Deseret
News* associates suffered a stroke, Mark took him for rides.
When one of the older Seventies was dying and his wife was
near collapse from her twenty-four-hour burden, Mark hired
a nurse to assist her. When another Seventy with a terminally
ill wife spent all he had on her care, Mark brought him the
keys to a new car parked at the curb, explaining, "This is for
you." When young men wanted to serve missions and their
families could not or would not afford the expense, Mark
paid their way. If a widow needed yard care or spending
money, Mark wrote a check. And always, he supported the
missionary fund; he would rather wear a shiny-seated suit
than shortchange his donations. Mark knew that without the
missionaries, he might never have been born in America;
that without the missionaries, his wife would probably have
remained in Great Britain. When he considered first things
first, it was the payment of missionary money over and above
his tithes and offerings that made him feel happiest. He left

no estate. He gave away all he had, laying up treasures where moth and rust could not touch them.

Mark's marvelous sense of humor rescued him from taking life too seriously. He never understood boredom and immersed himself in study. Whenever he was in town he went to the temple once a week. Poetry and literature, music, drama—all were familiar friends. He invented his own phonetic spelling system and wrote his private notes strictly by sound. Able to accept individuals without prejudice, he saw good in everyone. If a relative or acquaintance did not live the gospel, he thought no less of that person. His generosity seemed instinctive, and more often than not the gifts he received found their way to others. Integrity, kindness, love for the truth, courage, compassion, fairness—all were his, as was forgiveness, for there were those who had wronged him. Bearing no grudge, he prayed for their return to honesty and the Church.

15

World Travels

"This gospel shall be preached unto every nation"
(D&C 133:37)

The year 1980 was a very good year for Mark, and creating a stake in Nice, France, gave him great satisfaction. No one had expected to see the Latter-day Saints on the French Riviera, but with 1,755 members and a strong presidency, Nice Stake became a fact. Then he flew to Paris for a stake conference. At the conference, which was held at a theater in Versailles, he began a new study. For years he had interviewed patriarchs all over the Church to discover which tribes were being converted. Knowing that Ephraim was the believing blood, he found that most of the patriarchal blessings designated the new converts to be of Ephraim. In the midst of the conference at Versailles, with 1,032 people in attendance, Mark called the patriarchs out of the audience to ask them through interpreters just which peoples were received into membership. Then he launched into an inspired discourse on the manner in which the missionaries were to be led to believers. Following his talk, the Saints raised the rafters with "God Be with You Till We Meet Again," which brought tears to French and American eyes alike.

For an assignment to area conferences in the Orient, Mark traveled with President and Sister Kimball and President and Sister Hinckley. In the Philippine Islands, President Kimball and others in the group paid a courtesy call to Filipino President Marcos and were cordially received. A large auditorium with a metal roof had been rented for the area meetings, and some 15,000 Saints listened as the General Authorities instructed them in the truths of the gospel.

Mark seemed especially moved by the Spirit as he spoke. The lights directed at the podium gave his face a luminous appearance, and without taking his eyes from the audience, he spoke for an hour. No one moved. It seemed as if no one breathed. Suddenly a loud noise joined Mark's swelling voice, and someone softly said, "It is angels' wings." Actually, a rainstorm was pummeling the metal roof, but even if angels' wings had contributed to the sound, the Spirit could not have been stronger.

Often individuals feel some sort of crisis in their lives when a landmark birthday approaches. Turning thirty or forty or fifty seems to be an unforgettable experience, and stories are told of the depression accompanying the natal day. Mark neared his eightieth birthday as he traveled in the Orient. Bruce Lindsay, KSL anchorman, accompanied the tour and sent nightly news spots back to Salt Lake City. When he noticed Mark carrying his own luggage, Bruce tried to take the bag from his hand. Mark brushed him off in such an uncharacteristic way that Peggy, who accompanied Mark, asked if something were wrong. He replied, "Just because I am almost eighty doesn't mean I need help carrying a suitcase."

Another member of the group, Ed Burgoyne of Murdock Travel, knew of Mark's unwillingness to check his luggage. At every airport, Ed and his assistant counted bags, took them through customs, and personally brought the baggage to the hotel. While they were waiting for the plane to Korea, Ed approached Mark and suggested that as long as he personally handled the luggage, there was no reason for Mark to struggle with languages and officials. Mark reluctantly handed over his bag after first removing his scriptures, which he placed in an inside coat pocket. "Everything I own is in that suitcase," he explained to Ed, who again assured Mark that he personally counted every bag at every airport and placed each in the proper hotel room. In Korea, Ed counted the bags, went through customs, recounted the bags, and started for the hotel. When dinnertime approached, Mark wanted to change his shirt, so he called Ed's room. "When will the luggage arrive?" he asked. After a frantic search, Ed discovered to his horror that someone in the group had placed an extra piece of hand luggage on the pile at the airport, so that when he counted the bags, he had stopped before coming to the Petersen suitcase. A wild dash to the airport produced the missing valise, which sat forlornly alone in the middle of the arrival hall. No one had touched it. Nothing was missing. But Ed never again insisted that Mark check his luggage.

In Korea, the Saints' love for President Kimball warmed the chilly air. The morning conference meeting was held in a chapel, but the overflow crowd on the slopes around the building far outnumbered the number of persons inside. President Kimball's physician, Dr. Ernest Wilkinson, accompanied the Prophet, making sure that all went well healthwise. When President Kimball insisted that the afternoon session would take place out of doors, Dr. Wilkinson objected, pointing out that the Prophet was still recovering from recent surgery. President Kimball replied that if the people could survive out of doors in below zero weather, so could he. As the second meeting began, all the dignitaries sat on a stage outside, swathed in blankets and with heaters glowing at their feet.

Highlight of the conference was President Kimball's declaration that a temple would be built in Korea. An electric thrill vibrated through the audience as the Koreans realized the meaning of this announcement. Because of government regulations, an entire family could not leave Korea at the same time, so going to the Tokyo Temple for family sealings was impossible. With a temple in Korea, families would be able to be sealed for time and all eternity. After the meetings, when the visitors tried to drive away, so strong was the affection for President Kimball that the people crowded against the sides of the buses, hoping for a glimpse of him. Sensing their sorrow at his departure, he took a white handkerchief from his pocket and began waving to them. In response, a thousand handkerchiefs fluttered until the bus disappeared;

President Spencer W. Kimball greets Mark at general conference

then those same handkerchiefs wiped away tears of joy at the
opportunity to see a living prophet of the Lord. '

Conferences in Hong Kong, Taipei, Tokyo, and Osaka
each produced the same great uplifting feeling, as the Saints
of the Orient flocked to see their beloved leaders and hear
the words of truth. In his journal Mark wrote: "The people
were delighted just to see President Kimball. I should say
that a miracle really was performed in his behalf, because his
voice and his eyes and his vitality altogether improved tremendously so that he was able to carry the whole program
without any apparent difficulty. In each of the area conferences he spoke four times, and he spoke in each of the seven
sessions of the dedication of the temple in Tokyo in addition
to giving the dedicatory prayer."

An incident that Mark later described as one of the most
spiritual of his entire life occurred in the first session of the
Tokyo Temple dedication. The Spirit seemed to grow
stronger as the meeting progressed, and after the dedicatory
prayer and the Hosannah Shout led by President Kimball, the

choir sang the Evan Stephens hymn, "Hosannah, Hosannah, the House of the Lord Is Completed." Because the temple could not hold all who wanted to attend the dedication, the number of choir members had to be limited. The quality of voices in the choir was excellent, the expression and accuracy superb, but with so few singers, the volume was not loud. But when the choir began to sing, suddenly many, many voices joined them. Mark wrote: "It seemed that there was a far larger choir singing than was present, and various people thought there must have been an angelic choir singing with our little choir because of the beauty of the music and the volume that was heard. The Spirit was so strong that everybody burst into tears, including the members of the choir, who literally sang through their tears." Mark believed that the Oriental people on the other side felt such happiness at the thought of having their temple work done that they literally shouted and sang for joy.

While Mark was traveling to the temple dedication in the Far East, Ralph Rodgers was planning an eightieth birthday celebration for him in the twenty-sixth-floor dining room of the Church Office Building. The party was held shortly after his return. An original script illustrated by slides of very old pictures showed the Petersens from the time of Mark's mission. With Ralph and Pat Davis vocalizing songs appropriate to the period, whoops of laughter and ohs and ahs greeted the program. On the top of a large white sheet cake, Peggy and Drew reproduced in frosting the front page of the *Deseret News* announcing Mark's appointment to the Twelve. Surrounded by friends, family, and loved ones, Mark found the evening was not only a huge success but also a huge surprise.

A sentimental journey began when Mark and Peggy left for Nova Scotia to tour the Halifax Nova Scotia Mission. President and Sister James Kenning accompanied them as they visited places where Mark's mission had taken him. The itinerary involved traveling each morning, holding a missionary meeting in the afternoon, and participating in an investigator meeting in the evening. Mark's memories of a Halifax with only eight Latter-day Saints as he completed his mission contrasted sharply with the seven hundred Saints and investigators who jammed the little chapel and over-flowed outside. As in his talks sixty years before, he dis-cussed the Great Apostasy and the necessity for a restoration of the true church. Again he reiterated that the angel flying through the heavens bringing the everlasting gospel was to do so in the hour of God's judgment or in the last days. He told of the importance for investigators to find a modern church with prophets living today, for the Lord would do nothing without His servants the prophets. He explained that the members of that church should be called Saints, as he built his case for the truthfulness of The Church of Jesus Christ of Latter-day Saints.

Mark enjoyed showing his younger daughter the town clock on the hill where, as a missionary, he had climbed to see the view of the harbor and browse through the museum on preparation days. Walking around the walls of the Citadel, now part of a national historic park, he watched the ferry leaving its berth for Dartmouth and recalled the many times he had ridden a similar vessel to conduct street meetings. Now a mission home graced Dartmouth.

A trip into the past on Prince Edward Island with its gentle ways and quaint houses culminated in a rousing meeting of two hundred Saints and investigators. Then on to Saint John, New Brunswick, Canada's oldest incorporated city, known as the Liverpool of America. An enthusiastic crowd of three hundred met the man who had last visited the Bay of Fundy area without purse or scrip. Memories of blistered feet and broken beds and of testimonies borne to people who never seemed to listen flooded Mark's mind. Truro, the New Bruns-wick town that had almost defeated him—where he had tracted every door twice without being invited inside—now had a lovely Latter-day Saint chapel.

In Sydney, a reunion with Emma Marr's cousins, Donald and Marguerite Ferguson, added to the nostalgia of visiting her birthplace. Some two hundred persons assembled in the Sydney chapel to hear Mark speak of the Restoration. Donald and Marguerite took Peggy around the town and showed her the house where Emma and Sarah had stayed. The present owners allowed the trio to inspect the inside of the home and produced a land grant bearing the McDiarmid name. They visited the Sydney River, where Emma had won a medal for swimming, and the little church in which the minister had suggested that the McDonalds be ostracized. Picking up Mark after a missionary meeting, they drove around Glace Bay and the Sydney mines. Never had Emma Marr seemed closer to Mark since her death.

Mark's interest in the history of the American continent enhanced their visit to Newfoundland. It was believed that the Vikings landed on its shores in A.D. 1000. When Sir Humphrey Gilbert officially took possession of the island for Queen Elizabeth I in 1583, Newfoundland became Britain's oldest colony. A tour of the narrows, Fort Amherst, and Cabot Tower on Signal Hill, where Marconi received the first telegraphic message in 1901, pleased Mark as he prepared to speak to three hundred members and investigators.

Mark's trip was a journey into the past, and for a time his loneliness for Emma Marr seemed almost endurable. But seeing the Sydney where she was born, visiting with her relatives, and traveling to his old mission haunts where he had received her letters, all combined to bring his emotions very near the surface. In Canada not a day passed without his recalling the Shaws and their "Dare to be a Mormon." Mark E. Petersen had also dared to be a Mormon. He had dared to put the Church ahead of all his other interests. Now as he left Canada, thoughts of his beloved wife crowded his mind.

Soon after, a stake conference assignment called Mark to Chester, England, to the last place in the country to succumb to William the Conqueror. He wondered if it might also be the last place to succumb to Mormonism, but on meeting the mission and stake officers, he felt sure this was not so. As he walked around city walls dating from the fourteenth century (replacing earlier Norman and Roman structures), he imagined the men who came to found a military post in A.D. 48, the King's School established in 1541 by Henry VIII, the city's devastation by Llewellyn. Now a new army of young missionaries invaded the area, their modern dress contrasting with the half-timbered construction of the buildings. Mark knew that the message they carried was older than creation, yet it offered a newness of life and fulfillment of purpose. He prayed that these young—and some not so young—men and women would study and labor, becoming profitable servants. When he met with the missionaries, he realized that they had been well trained in the scriptures. As he surveyed the ancient scene, he thought about the time when the missionaries would return to their homes after their missions, noting that the future of the Church rested on their willingness to stay involved in the work.

The following weekend he was to visit the Poole England Stake. Between the two stake conferences, President A. Harold Goodman in London put him to good use in meetings with the missionaries. An investigator fireside at Hyde Park Chapel attracted a record crowd and brought back memories of the time when Mark and Emma had lived in Great Britain.

By the time the Poole Stake conference officially began, Mark's enthusiasm over the possibilities for work in England had reached a high pitch. Wherever he spoke, converts from his time as mission president crowded the pulpit afterwards. Most told of their joy in the gospel, but occasionally he heard from inactives who had come out only because they knew him. He wondered how many prospective and inactive members he might attract at each town if he could return and "whistle stop" throughout the country. If he traveled in the mornings, met with local city and Church officials in the afternoon, and held a mass meeting at night, he believed he could blanket the country in two months and do a great deal of good.

A touching letter waited on Mark's desk at home. The au-

President Ezra Taft Benson, left; Elders Mark E. Petersen,
Delbert L. Stapley, LeGrand Richards

thor, a bishop's wife, recalled his visit to their stake conference when she was a child. As he spoke on the importance of
morality, he had reached into a bouquet of flowers on the
stand and, apologizing to flower lovers in the audience, removed one perfect rose from the arrangment. He pulled a
petal from the bloom and showed that losing one petal had
caused little damage. Then one by one the petals fell from
the stem until nothing lovely was left. His point had been that
each dishonest or immoral act takes away from the whole.
She had never forgotten. He was grateful to receive her note,
for sometimes he wondered if all the traveling and all the
talking really made difference.

During the early part of 1983, stake conferences took
Mark from one end of the nation to the other until April general conference, which fell on Easter weekend. He delivered
a classic talk on Easter, speaking on the life and mission of
the Savior. That evening, the rededication of the Assembly
Hall on Temple Square was held in the midst of a heavy
spring snowstorm. As one of the speakers, Mark reminisced
about events significant to him that had taken place in that

edifice. He spoke emotionally of the weekly gatherings of the Danish members, meetings that had been so important to his parents. A strange land, a strange language, a new religion—nothing mattered as the Danish Saints shared the strength of their convictions each Sunday. Emma Marr had taken organ lessons in the Assembly Hall. As he described the wonderful structural improvements in the renovated hall, he commented on the magnificent new organ. "But," he added, "I loved the old organ that served for so many years in this building—because her hands had touched those keys."

Following the conference, Mark received a letter complimenting him on his great testimony of the Savior and telling the following anecdote: "The eight-hour taxi ride we took together from Sao Paulo to Londrina was especially important to me. Every Church member dreams of the day he can ask the questions of his heart of an apostle. To sit by your side without interruption from telephones and other outside distractions was a dream come true. I know you were in great pain because of your recent knee operation. Never a word of complaint, only patience and encouragement for a struggling mission president. As we checked into the hotel in Londrina, I felt impressed to tell the clerk that he was registering an apostle of the Lord, one of only twelve such men on earth. I told him that you would be speaking the next day, and Sunday would be the only opportunity for him to hear an apostle. He replied that he had to work. I told him that hearing you was more important than working; he must attend. He said he would try. About six months later he sought me out after a mission conference. He had attended the conference in which you created the Londrina Stake. He said that as he listened to you speak, the Spirit bore witness that he was listening to an apostle of the Lord. He contacted the missionaries, was baptized, and had prepared himself to serve a full-time mission."

An assignment to New Zealand and Australia in the spring of 1983 provided Mark with some exciting moments, starting with his check-in at the airport. Peggy was to accompany him, and at the Western Airlines desk in Salt Lake City, her reservation was confirmed but Mark's failed to appear on the computer. They managed to get to Los Angeles, where Peggy's daughter Sydney and her husband, Bob Bennion, took them on a tour of the harbor in their sailboat, with Grandpa Mark wearing the only suit he possessed for the next two weeks. Spray flew over the bow as he thought how Sydney sailed her boat the way her grandmother had driven her car. After a lunch of fish and chips on the dock, they headed for the airport. But when Mark checked in, he discovered that through some error, all his reservations from Salt Lake to Auckland to Australia and back again had been cancelled. The flight to Auckland was now fully booked.

Mark explained to the agent manning the computer that an urgent meeting waited in Hamilton. Finally the agent called his boss, who called his boss, who called his boss, who found a seat for Mark in the smoking section. Sitting in a smoking area on a short hop for one who is unaccustomed to tobacco is a throat-choking, eye-watering experience. An overseas flight in a smoking section is all of the above—only much longer. But Mark thanked the Qantas employees and boarded the plane. Peggy was able to exchange her seat for one next to her father, and the ordeal began.

As the air thickened, Peggy thought what a very nice man her father was. Though nearly eighty-three, he had worked feverishly at the office to prepare for his committee assignments and the conferences, written some *Church News* editorials, outlined a book of Bible stories for children, found his flight reservations cancelled, gone for a sail and eaten fish from a newspaper, and now sat in the back of a cabin filled with blue smoke—with a smile on his face, looking forward to New Zealand.

As part of the schedule, a session in the New Zealand Temple was held. When Mark arrived, the first couple from New Guinea ever to be endowed had just completed their marriage ceremony. This occasion, combined with the presence of a member of the Twelve, completely overwhelmed

the facilities. Extra folding chairs had been placed on a balcony, and many of the men stood throughout the endow-
ment.

After the meeting, Mark and Peggy drove to Auckland for
a regional fireside for married couples. Mark gave a talk on
astronomy, explaining the vastness of space and the powers
of Christ as Creator. He pointed out the locations of planets
and galaxies with a wave of the arm, pacing back and forth on
the stand, hating to be restricted to one small space. After the
meeting he shook a thousand hands, as the Saints crowded
around him.

Flying to Australia, Mark and Peggy excitedly discussed
the coming mission tour, where they would be the guests of
Ned and Gwen Winder. Mark had worked with Ned in the
Church Missionary Department, and he explained to his
daughter that for a time Ned *was* the Missionary Department.

At Adelaide, they could see the Winders waiting for them.
President Ned had presided previously over the Florida Mission, before going to work for the Missionary Department.
Occasionally the Winders were called to preside in a mission
for a short term when a mission president was ill or had been
reassigned. Gwen Winder loved people and was able to adjust to varied living conditions with what appeared to be
great ease. Great missionaries, the Winders found joy in the
service of the Lord. And wherever they went, the Saints loved
them as soon as they met them. Now, with happy anticipation, Mark approached his visit with the Winders to Whyalla,
Marian and Modbury stakes in Adelaide, and Mildura District
in the state of Victoria.

The drive to Whyalla, a district of the Adelaide Mission,
proved to be fascinating for Mark, who delighted in the an-
tics of the kangaroos and brief glimpses of koalas nearly hidden by the gum tree leaves on which they lived. A flock of
imus ran along the parched earth beside the car. Scattered
houses with wraparound porches to shade their owners from
an unforgiving sun nestled in green oases in the desert.

As the party journeyed toward Whyalla, so the Saints in

the area were driving toward the scheduled meeting, some traveling a day and a half, sleeping on floors of the members' homes at night, in order to hear an apostle testify of Christ. At the meetinghouse in Whyalla, the excitement and good-will of the waiting members greeted the tired visitors, who joined district officers for a many-course meal in the Relief Society room. The meeting that followed was emotional and uplifting as spirit met spirit in the love of the work. Mark stood and told all the reasons why the light of Christ should enter each heart, telling the Saints that "Jesus indeed was sent from heaven by His Father, that He is the Savior, that the gospel must be lived in word, in conversation, in charity, in spirit, in faith, and in purity." He spoke of the sacred nature of baptism and of the sacrament. "The cross is not the symbol of Christ," he declared. "We remember not a Christ crucified but a Christ who now lives for us just as He died for us."

As Mark bore witness to the divine ministry of the Savior, the listening Saints, tears streaming down their faces, trea-sured every word. At last they sat in the same room with a member of the Twelve. The brotherhood of the gospel, the joys of the message, the hope of eternal life, and a visitor from the headquarters of the Church combined to over-whelm them.

In the mission district of Mildura, Victoria, buffet tables groaning with Australian delicacies waited in the cultural hall when the Winders and Petersens entered the church. The women had prepared their specialities, and each wanted to give a portion to Elder Petersen. The Saints sat in family groups and parents made sure each child shook the visitor's hand. Word came that a newspaper reporter waited in the foyer for an interview. Mark discovered it was the mayor's daughter, a very green journalism major, reminding him of his early days at the *Deseret News*. Mark knew how difficult it was to face an editor when an assignment had not gone well and information was sketchy, so he patiently answered each query. President Winder learned later that the resulting publicity strengthened the Church's position in Mildura, assuring a friendly greeting for tracting missionaries.

A combined meeting of the Modbury and Marian stakes drew a standing-room-only crowd of nearly two thousand, not including those sitting on the grass beneath the open windows. Mark reveled in the strength of the Church in the area.

On their final day in Adelaide, Mark and Peggy joined the Winders for lunch at the mission home, where colorful native birds lived in the backyard. Then they all drove up the mountain to Cleland National Park. Dingoes peered from their dens, koalas drowsed in the sun, and wallabyes and kangaroos wandered aimlessly, all enjoying the warm day. One very old, lame kangaroo attracted Mark's attention. Mark commented that there were days when he knew just how that old kangaroo felt. The others laughed as they remembered the energy Mark had expended during the past week, enduring long rides, stifling heat, and strange motels, endless handshaking, interviews, and talks. As he thanked the Winders and boarded his plane, Mark pronounced the Adelaide experience one of his all-time best mission tours.

If Mark had foreseen that he was in the last year of his life, he might have wanted to go three places: to Denmark, the homeland of his parents; to Great Britain, where he had lived and worked; and to Israel, to follow the footsteps of the Christ. He was able to visit all three areas.

On a cold, drizzly day in the second week of June 1983, Mark flew to Copenhagen to reorganize the stake presidency. The affection he felt for the Danes radiated from his eyes as he greeted the congregation in Danish. When he discovered that the mission president was the son of a childhood friend, his joy was complete. The youth and vitality of the stake thrilled him. Occasionally a meeting will be so filled with the warmth of the Spirit that members and investigators alike rejoice in the gospel of Christ. Such an experience took place in Copenhagen. On overseas trips Mark always attempted to crowd several miles of walking into the schedule to make up for all the sitting on the plane and in meetings. As he strolled the streets of Copenhagen each day, he had a feeling of coming home.

Following the conference, Mark flew to London, where he was welcomed by President and Sister Goodman. Various missionary and investigator meetings were to fill the week, followed by the stake conference at Newcastle-under-Lyme. President Goodman had scheduled an investigator meeting, and Mark felt exhilarated as he viewed the largest crowd he had ever seen at Hyde Park Ward. As he rose to speak, drawing his little New Testament from his coat pocket, he looked out at those assembled, squinted as if appraising their level of interest, and then launched into possibly the greatest missionary sermon of his life. Those sitting on the stand watched members of the audience flipping the pages of their Bibles with Mark as he bore his witness of the truth. The unwavering gaze of investigators bore into him as they sought answers. Through the hour of his talk, those standing never changed positions. The little boy on the front row didn't make a sound. The power of Mark's testimony vibrated across the chapel as he assured his listeners that he knew of the reality of the Savior.

That fall Mark was assigned to participate in a BYU Travel Study cruise of the Mediterranean, accompanied by Peggy. As the group boarded barges at the Venice airport for the trip by water to the city center, Mark was pleased to see how many people on the tour he already knew. Surrounded by friendly faces, he enjoyed his trip down the Grand Canal and then wandering in the crooked streets of the city. San Marcos Square with its fascinating clock and as many pigeons as tourists reminded him of his last trip to Venice with Emma Marr. How she would have enjoyed this trip, he thought, as he boarded the *MTS Danae*, which would be his home for the next two weeks.

The first stop, in Dubrovnik, Yugoslavia, established a pattern for the following ports of call. Mark managed to extricate Dr. Richard Gunn, BYU Travel Study expert, from the rest of the group, and together the two men examined the old city wall and the town square. Mark was especially interested in the churches. From the time he had lived in Europe, his search for confirmation of the practice of baptism by immersion in the early church had been rewarded with some excellent finds of baptismal fonts. Dick Gunn possessed the kind of mind Mark most appreciated, and the excitement of discovery dominated their time together.

After two days at sea, the ship docked at Alexandria, Egypt. Buses and limousines met the ship and loaded up for the drive to Cairo. As the limousines carrying Mark and other special guests and speakers reached the outskirts of Cairo, a drunk driver, pursued by a motorcycle policeman, careened across the road, narrowly missing the lead limousine but heading straight for the one in which Mark rode. The limousine driver pulled at the wheel with such force that his shirt split down the back, and the limousine spun off the road, coming to a bumpy stop along the shoulder. The passengers breathed a sign of relief that there had been no collision. But later, at the hotel in Cairo, Peggy's ankle began to swell, and Mark found himself in pain and wondering if he had reinjured his broken rib. He was taking blood-thinning drugs, and the slightest bump or injury is potentially dangerous, but it did not occur to Mark that after the jolt, he was bleeding internally.

While the rest of the group toured Cairo and the tombs, rode camels, and wandered through the splendor of King Tut's collection at the Cairo Museum, Mark rested in his room. That night he was unable to sleep. Lying down increased his discomfort, and he couldn't find a comfortable position in a chair. After pacing the floor, moving to the bed, then the chair, then pacing again, he finally tried to locate Dr. Russell M. Nelson, who was with the cruise group. The switchboard operator told him that there wasn't a person by that name registered in the hotel. Finally, through Peggy, Dr. Nelson was located. He examined Mark and probed, but he couldn't locate the source of the problem. Then, in the gray of early dawn and with muffled traffic noises already heralding the day outside, Dr. Nelson placed his hands on the head of the suffering apostle and gave him a priesthood blessing.

Already the *Danae* seemed like home, and Mark gratefully returned to his bed there, sleeping the sleep of the just. The next stop, Ashdod, Israel, was the port closest to Jerusalem. For three days the tour group would be taken by bus into Jerusalem, returning to the ship at night.

On Saturday, the Jewish Sabbath, Mark was scheduled to meet some of the local Latter-day Saints for lunch, inspect the site of the new BYU center and library on the Mount of Olives, visit the Orson Hyde Memorial Park, then drive to Shepherd's Field, where sacrament meeting was to be held. As he returned to the familiar scenes of the mount, the Garden Tomb, and Gethsemane, Mark was overwhelmed with emotion. And once again he wished his beloved Emma Marr were with him, to see again these sacred places they had first visited so long ago.

At Shepherd's Field, the night was clear but cold, and the rocks on which the audience sat were hard. Lights twinkled in Bethlehem in the distance, and ragged Arab children herded sheep and goats along a rough track nearby. As a chorus of BYU Semester Abroad students began to sing, the listeners knew how sweetly the angels had sounded in that sacred place two thousand years before. By the time the sacrament was passed and the other speakers had finished, Mark felt that the shivering crowd should be released from their misery. Thus, as he had done in the Tabernacle those many years ago, he rose and quickly bore his humble but fervent testimony as a special witness, then sat down.

Two days later, on the Mount of Beatitudes, Mark enjoyed a picnic lunch in the warm sun. With the only sounds coming from birds and insects, he tried to imagine the countryside as it had been in the time of Christ. Then standing with his feet planted on the ground where Jesus had walked, one hand holding his scriptures, the other a microphone, he gave forceful sermons to two separate groups of the Saints.

Through the kindness of David Galbraith and Kelly Ogden, who directed the BYU Semester Abroad program in Israel, Mark experienced the highlight of his trip. He had never been to the top of Mount Tabor, the Mount of Transfiguration, the site where Peter, James, and John received the keys to the priesthood and where, as His three disciples watched, Christ was transfigured and conversed with Moses and Elijah. It is reported that Peter offered to make three tabernacles—for the Lord, Moses, and Elias—and in commemoration of this, the Catholics had built on the mountain a lovely church with three chapels. Kelly Ogden, who has a lovely tenor voice, received permission from the priest in charge and sang a Jewish chant in front of the three chapels. So strong was the Spirit that tourists wandering through the area stopped to listen, fascinated by the small ceremony they witnessed.

As the ship set sail for Ephesus, Mark wished he felt better. But he decided that regardless of any health problem, he would speak in the amphitheater where the beloved apostle Paul had spoken so often. As he viewed Ephesus for the first time since the archaeological restoration of the ancient city, he was amazed at the vast work that had been accomplished. On a previous trip he had played author and photographer and sent an article to the *Improvement Era* documenting the baptismal fonts found there. Now he walked down stone streets still bearing the marks of chariot wheels and saw the public baths, the library, the temples all recently excavated. He truly thrilled at his visit to Paul's city.

In the amphitheater, standing where Paul had stood, Mark slowly opened his New Testament. But having just completed writing his book *The Teachings of Paul*, he did not need to read from the open book in his hand as he explained the doctrines of the ancient apostle. With steady voice he bore testimony to the truth of Paul's words. Many in the audience reported that a bright light seemed to glow from his face. The local Turkish guides wept and said that they had never before heard such power and simplicity. When he sat down and the cruise choir sang its final number, echoes of heavenly music trembled on the air.

Each day Mark's pallor increased and his ability to tolerate food decreased. He no longer bounded up stairs but leaned heavily on his companions as he waited for elevators. Still, Mars Hill at the base of the Acropolis beckoned. Like Alma, Mark could not rest, but went forth preaching. On a cold, breezy day, he spoke to each of the ten or so BYU bus groups as they arrived at the hill. Because of the wind, the listeners crowded around him in order to catch each word. At such close range they could see the extra pages of references that he had glued into his copy of the New Testament. Following his formal speech, he answered questions about his methods of cross-referencing his Bible. Then, after the last group disappeared down the trail, he gratefully sank onto a bench and took one last long look at the scene of Paul's speech on the "unknown God," commenting that he had written a book on that subject once.

No record of the travels of the modern-day Paul, the apostle Mark E. Petersen, would be complete without mentioning his use of time, especially during flights or waiting at an airport for connections. He always had a book to read or a manuscript to work on. His briefcase never left home without some volume that excited him. He had no time for fiction; he preferred to read books of scripture, biography, history, and science.

Because of his interest in the places he visited, coupled with his grasp of current events, his mind overflowed with fascinating facts, which made mealtimes memorable learning experiences for his companions. After his death, those close to him found themselves still marking articles and passages that they thought would interest him, then hurrying down the hall to share with him, forgetting that he would not be sitting in his favorite chair, poring over a book.

16

Illness and Death

"Though he slay me, yet will I trust him"
(Job 13:15)

During most of his life, except for the nagging back pain, Mark enjoyed excellent health. Elevators were always too slow for him. When he worked at the *Deseret News*, he never merely walked up the stairs—he always took them at a run, two at a time. At the Church offices, he'd park his car in the underground garage and then dash two flights up the stairs to his office. In the last decade of his life, however, one affliction after another came upon him, presenting trials and suffering that might have broken the spirit of a lesser man. Not so Mark Petersen. Though he had great physical pain and afflictions that might be likened unto those of Job, he continued to enrich his mind and to be about his Father's business.

In the fall of 1976, with three stake conferences scheduled in England, Mark checked into his favorite London hotel, the Rembrandt. The elevator, like the hotel itself, was very old-fashioned. It ran on water pressure—and unfortunately, London was experiencing a severe water shortage. Thus Mark had to climb the ten flights to go to and from his room. He noticed that it seemed harder than usual to climb the steps.

When he returned home in late November, he dreaded entering his home on Diestel Road for the first time. While he was away the thermostat had been set at 50 degrees, and the chill in the air matched the cold, lonely feeling that greeted him as he opened the door. All his life he had depended on getting at least seven hours of sleep, in order to

*Mark at the
Visitors' Center
on Temple Square*

continue the terrific pace he set for himself. Now jet lag seemed overpowering, and after carefully stepping over the stack of mail on the floor by the front door, he was grateful to fall into bed.

The next day Mark was alarmed to discover that he had begun to hemorrhage heavily during the night. He called his doctor and was told to go immediately to the hospital. The problem that had first reared its ugly head while Mark was mission president at White Hayes had reappeared.

On December 1, 1976, diagnostic surgery was performed. Not only was there a malignancy, but the cells were anaplastic, a most virulent form of carcinoma. The cancer had apparently spread to some lymph nodes, so further surgery was performed.

After Mark was released from the hospital to go to Peggy's home for recovery, the specter of cancer lurked in his mind as well as the minds of his family. Of all those involved, Mark seemed least concerned. He explained the the Lord could have him anytime He wanted, but meanwhile Mark was going to continue doing His work. As soon as he was able, he moved back to his own home and started radiation treatments at the University Hospital. He received treatments four or five times a week for eight weeks.

A stake conference in Midvale, Utah, was Mark's first assignment following his illness. He had felt languid all week, a condition to which he had never been accustomed. He wrote in his journal: "I went to the Lord and told him of the problem I was having and that I needed strength to handle the conference assignment in Midvale. It was just miraculous! I felt as though I had never been sick. I conducted the Saturday meetings we had outlined, and on Sunday morning a split session, one at 9 A.M. and the second at 11 A.M. I attended all of the meetings and felt perfectly well. The Lord surely was with me. After I had returned to my home Sunday evening, I again felt very tired, and the strength I had experienced during the conference left me. How glad I was to get back into the work again!"

Mark's condition continued to improve, and when he returned for his first monthly checkup following completion of his radiation treatments, his doctor was pleased with his progress. His good health and boundles energy carried him from early morning until late at night, and he was able to continue to work at the office all week as well as reorganize stakes on weekends.

When a pain in his right knee persisted in slowing his charge up the stairs of the Church Administration Building and occasionally forced him to use an elevator, he agreed to try a new surgical procedure to remedy the situation. On September 30, 1979, at the conclusion of a fireside talk in Provo, his family drove him to Cottonwood Hospital in Salt Lake County, where he was admitted for surgery on the cartilege in his right knee. What would formerly have meant six weeks in a cast and enormous pain had now been simplified through microsurgery, with almost immediate recovery of the patient. The surgery was performed early Monday morning, and by one o'clock that afternoon, with no lunch forthcoming, Mark announced he was going home—and he did! He attended meetings at seven the next morning and was able to continue through the heavy general conference schedule that week with no need for pain medication. The only unpleasant aspect of the experience was having his doctor accuse him of having old knees. The physician was quick to add, however, that Mark's knees were the only old part of him, and Mark was satisfied.

For the next three years, Mark continued to enjoy good health and to carry on his assignments in the Lord's work. Then, in July 1982, he was afflicted again, this time with pneumonia and a blood clot in his lung. Confined to bed, he still found time to do his office work with Dorene shuttling mail and problems between the Church Administration Building and the hospital.

Following Mark's release from the hospital, Dr. James Webster continued to visit him every day at home, ostensibly social calls, but also, he told the family, to make sure the recovery went as it should. Now he pronounced Mark cured and gave him permission to attend stake conference in Carson City, Nevada, where he was to reorganize the stake presidency. The following Saturday Peggy received a call from Dr. Webster's wife, Gwen. The previous evening Jim had been on a training parachute jump near Camp Williams, in the southern part of Salt Lake County. He had completed the exercise with his usual soft landing, but while he was walking back to camp along a dirt road, an impatient teenager swerved around a slower car and hit Jim, killing him instantly.

Now Peggy must decide whether to disturb her father's conference in Nevada or take a chance that, unable to sleep, he might turn on the radio and hear a newscast. When she reached him, he was already aware that something was wrong with Jim Webster. He had dreamed that night that Jim had gone.

Still shaken from pneumonia and shock, Mark spoke at the funeral services. Recalling his association with Dr. Webster, he told of the physician's influence on his grandchildren and of the time Jim had literally saved Mark's own life after back surgery. Then, in matter-of-fact tones, he told of an interview that Jim had just experienced with the Savior in which he was asked how he had treated his fellowmen. In the audience was Jim's associate, Dr. Russell M. Nelson, who would later be called to serve in the Council of the Twelve Apostles. He wrote to Mark, "Having just returned from the funeral service for our dear friend and colleague, Dr. James W. Webster, I want you to know how moved and inspired we all were to have heard your address at his funeral service. I happened to be sitting by many not of our faith, including Jews, Catholics, Protestants, and the like. I testify to you that there wasn't one of them who wasn't moved to the point of conviction that they had heard a true apostle of the Lord speak to them."

When Emma Marr had begun to have a series of strokes that changed her personality as well as affected her comprehension, Mark believed that if it could happen to her, it could happen to anyone. She had been so mentally alert and gifted, and to see her deteriorate before his eyes was extremely painful. The one fear he felt was that he might follow the same route and become senile. Over and over he made his secretary and his family promise that if his mental condition ever diminished to the point where he could not work, they should lock him away from prying eyes and not let anyone visit him. As he continued to carry on his heavy responsibilities well into his eighties, if he received any blessing, it was that his very young, very sharp mind remained alert to the end.

The year 1983 brought recurrences of several health problems. In June, following stake conference in Copenhagen, Mark traveled to London, where he prepared for a stake conference. But shortly after his arrival, he began to hemorrhage during the night. He was staying at the apartment of President and Sister Goodman and did not want to disturb them, so he waited until morning to inform them of his trouble. A call was placed to his physician in Salt Lake City, and he advised Mark to return home as soon as possible. Mark took the next plane out. When the plane finally touched down in Salt Lake City, Dorene had arranged for a Church security officer to help him off the plane and to the hospital immediately.

Extensive tests and scans were taken, followed by surgery. Mark spent most of the summer recuperating at home. He wrote in his journal, "While I was confined to home, I felt well enough to work but couldn't move around much, so I wrote three manuscripts—*The Teachings of Paul, The Sons of Mosiah,* and *The Jaredites.* I had previously written a manuscript titled *Alma and Abinadi.*" The latter book was already in production and would be released that fall.

In September Mark felt well enough to address a fireside at Brigham Young University. A neighbor who watched a rebroadcast of the speech told him she thought the tape had been made at least ten years earlier, because Mark seemed so vigorous. As he drove home from the fireside, he commented on how well he felt and how he had been blessed with recovery. He could run up and down stairs at work, and instead of sending interoffice mail to his colleagues or letting Dorene deliver it, he often made deliveries himself. He chuckled as he related that occasionally one of the younger General Authorities seemed startled that Mark would visit his office instead of sending a messenger. But he enjoyed doing things his way, and he injected as much exercise as possible into his days.

That fall, with his health and energy level approaching normal, Mark looked forward to both general conference and his assignment to lecture during the BYU Travel Study cruise of the Mediterranean. The Monday morning of con-

President Ezra Taft Benson and Elder Mark E. Petersen

ference week, he decided to paint some outside doors and window frames at home. Tuesday night, trying to relieve his aching muscles, he twisted in bed. The resulting pain was excruciating, and he wondered if he had reinjured his spine. He went to work on Wednesday but stayed home in bed on Thursday and Friday. On Saturday, October 1, he attended both conference sessions. After the morning meeting, President Gordon B. Hinckley suggested that Mark go home, so obvious was his distress. But he wanted to give his talk, which was scheduled for the afternoon session, so he declined the suggestion. At 3:15 P.M., when he addressed the conference, only great determination and courage allowed him to speak through his pain. Following the meeting, Peggy called Mark's doctor, who met them at the hospital. An X ray revealed a broken rib.

When Mark's pain continued to be almost intolerable, he wondered whom he could call at the last minute to substitute for him on the cruise assignment. Then, a few days after conference, Elder Boyd K. Packer stopped in and Mark explained that he could stand the pain no longer. Nothing seemed to relieve his distress, and for the first time he felt that he could not go on. Elder Packer placed his hands on Mark's head and rebuked the pain. Almost immediately Mark was healed.

On October 14, with the approval and encouragement of his doctors, Mark, accompanied by Peggy, left Salt Lake City to fly to Venice, where the cruise would begin. When he learned that Dr. Russell M. Nelson and some twenty other physicians planned to conduct a medical seminar as the ship sailed between ports, he relaxed and began to look forward to the talks he had been assigned. After the accident in Cairo, his condition deteriorated, but he decided that he would endure to the end of the cruise. By the time the cruise was over and the airplane reached Salt Lake City, Peggy rushed to the nearest phone and called Mark's physician, Dr. David Kimball. He suggested a blood test on the way home.

Early the next morning a very sick Mark Petersen entered the hospital, where blood poisoning was diagnosed as the cause of his discomfort. The doctors explained that with the amount of poison in his system, most people would have drifted into unconsciousness and quietly died in their sleep. Mark, however, had stood in the cold wind on Mars Hill, preaching the gospel.

A new medical procedure was attempted, and Mark underwent surgery under local anesthetic. During his hospitalization, many of his colleagues from 47 East South Temple stopped briefly to wish him well. He brightened perceptibly whenever a member of the Twelve arrived. Elder Packer visited daily, sometimes twice a day, and he and Elders Thomas S. Monson and James E. Faust each just happened to enter Mark's room at times when he badly wanted blessings. Elder and Sister Marvin J. Ashton stopped in on their way to the South Pacific, and the family of Elder Charles Didier brought best wishes and an enormous bouquet of flowers. Others also came, and President Gordon B. Hinckley called regularly.

As Mark's blood chemistry returned to the normal range, he once again itched to get back in harness. He and Peggy worked on the Bible stories, which he hoped would convert parents as they read to children. Every day he studied the two daily Salt Lake City newspapers, comparing their coverage of stories, checking for typographical errors, repeated words, and other items of interest to an ex-newspaperman. Every day he listened to national and local newscasts, commenting on the quality of the coverage. He read news magazines, astronomy and science magazines, and, of course, Church publications. He continued these reading habits and wrote *Church News* editorials as well.

Until the time of Emma Marr's death, Mark had never experienced major illness. Now, in close succession, he had had several surgeries and illnesses. He never complained, and when hospital employees, nervous because he was a "celebrity," tried to draw blood or perform some other service with shaking hands, he would smile in reassurance. The only indication of the depth of his suffering was the extra amount of time he spent with his bedroom door closed, telling his Father of his distress. His reading increased. He searched for answers in Job and in the trials of the Prophet Joseph Smith. Occasionally, alone with a family member, he wondered aloud why he was in the crucible. But he never doubted, never lost perspective, never failed to see some humor in his condition, never ceased learning, never became bitter.

Mark chose to ignore his physical problems. When well-intentioned acquaintances offered sympathy, he told them the cancer didn't matter. He was in his Father's hands and couldn't be bothered with worry. When an astonished physician who read his hospital charts following the cruise told Mark that his blood chemistry was so bad that he should be dead or at least unconscious, Mark replied quietly, "I was supposed to give those talks." His concern with his body related to his ability to do his work well. Any distress or discomfort was tolerable if he could be about his Father's business.

December 6, 1983, a red-letter day on Mark's calendar, saw him return to the office for the first time in two months. "I hope to be able to come down for a little while each day now to build up my strength," he wrote in his journal. When the snow became heavy and the roads almost impassable, he delighted in driving to work in a little four-wheel-drive truck.

On December 16, Mark wrote, "Today I was able to attend a special meeting of the Twelve. Some of the brethren picked me up at home and drove me downtown for this special meeting. I was delighted to be able to go." Afterwards he told his family, "I needed to be in that meeting. It was one of the most important of my life. Afterward almost everyone came to tell me how glad he was that I had expressed my opinion. This is a difficult time for Gordon Hinckley, who carries so much of the burden of the Church. He is doing a magnificent job, just as I would expect."

During the holidays Mark continued to go to the Church office daily even though it was technically closed for Christmas vacation. When he insisted on keeping his appointment that week for tithing settlement, Peggy waited in the drafty hall outside the bishop's office, wondering what Mark and Bishop Oliver Johnston could be discussing for thirty minutes. Mark later explained that he had instructed the bishop to reemphasize spirituality in sacrament meetings. A few months earlier, he had made a film on the meaning of the sacrament, and he hoped that the members of the Church would be aware of the sanctity of this holy ordinance.

But Mark's outward vigor and spirit concealed inner physical problems. In his journal he wrote, "I have been nauseous for the last few weeks. Because Peggy and the rest of the family have had a bout with the flu, I thought that was also what I had. Today I went to the doctor, who determined that my gall bladder was not functioning properly. Therefore, they will put me into the hospital."

As Peggy drove Mark to the hospital, they discussed the possibility of his barnstorming Great Britain the next summer, visiting missionaries, investigators, and members and

President Gordon B. Hinckley and Mark

firing them up with the spirit of the gospel. He wanted especially to visit remote areas where the faithful saw few General Authorities. He felt that he knew the people well enough
to be able to motivate them to greater activity. "After all," he
said, smiling, "I lived with your British mother successfully
for over fifty years."

No thought of death entered Mark's mind or the minds of
his family as he approached gall-bladder surgery. Except for
the nausea, he felt fairly well. When Elder Monson stopped at
the hospital on his way to a stake conference, he gave Mark a
blessing, asking that all connected with his care would be
skillful. The two men, who were almost like father and son,
discussed the coming ordeal without dread. Mark explained
that he just wanted to get the operation over with and go
back to work. When Dr. Philip Clark, one of his doctors,
came in, he told him, "I'm going to lick this, Phil. I know this
is the answer, and I am going to win!"

On Monday, January 9, when the orderly brought the

gurney to take him to the operating room, Mark smiled and waved, saying he wouldn't be long. The surgery apparently went well, and the surgeons felt relieved that the cancer apparently hadn't spread. But just to make sure, they had taken a biopsy of Mark's liver. Mark was returned to his room, where he peacefully slept off the anesthetic. But as Peggy watched throughout the day, she became concerned. Though he was in no pain and was able to answer intelligently when she spoke to him, he constantly drifted off to sleep. When she offered to turn on the evening news, for the first time in her life she heard her father say he didn't care about the news.

That night Mark was moved to intensive care, where tests indicated neither liver nor kidney function. And in the morning, when results of the biopsy came in, they showed that Mark had no liver—it was all one big tumor. Family members were called, and several members of the Twelve stopped in briefly. On Wednesday, when Elders Boyd K. Packer and A. Theodore Tuttle gave him a blessing, Mark smiled and said, "That's just what I needed." But mostly he drifted off in sleep.

At four o'clock that afternoon the Twelve met to form a prayer circle in Mark's behalf. Six hours later, at 10:22 P.M., surrounded by his family, Mark Edward Petersen passed away. His grandson Mark was the last person he spoke to. He looked at the young man and repeated, as he had from the youth's earliest childhood, "Let's stick together."

To his loved ones gathered at his bedside, Mark had always been a true patriarch. Whenever they had a problem, a need to talk, a disappointment or triumph to be shared, it was to their father and grandfather that they had gone. He had always been there, filled with love and encouragement, never judging, yet poking holes in unnecessarily inflated egos, gently teaching them to laugh at themselves. Now they finally began to accept the fact that he had chosen to leave them. He had wanted above all else to remain sharp and active to the end, to serve the Lord and mankind as long as he could, to not be a burden or to have to suffer with diminished mental capacity or ability. Now, as they watched through their tears, the machinery measuring his vital signs told them that a kind Heavenly Father had given him his wish.

Mark's journal concludes with this passage from Doctrine and Covenants 42:46: "And it shall come to pass that those who die in me shall not taste of death, for it *shall be sweet* unto them." This scripture was fulfilled literally at Cottonwood Hospital on January 11, 1984.

For the past forty years, since he had become a member of the Council of the Twelve, Mark had met with the families of deceased General Authorities to help plan their funerals. Now, without him, Elders Monson and Packer sat in the Barton living room deciding on funeral prayers, speakers, and music. Elder Monson recalled a similar occasion when, as they were leaving a family meeting, Mark had ordered him never to schedule his funeral in the Salt Lake Tabernacle. "No one would come," he explained.

He was wrong. The Tabernacle was filled to capacity with individuals whose lives Mark had touched. In spite of ill health, President Kimball and President Romney sat on the stand and listened to the speakers describe their beloved friend and associate as a man of integrity, honor, loyalty, love, and devotion. President Hinckley stated that Mark "literally wore out his life in traveling over the earth testifying of the divinity of the Lord Jesus Christ as the Son of the living God." President Ezra Taft Benson declared, "He never slackened his pace, notwithstanding infirmities or illness." "Elder Petersen was a giant of a man, a man of modesty, a man of ability, a man of love, and a man of God," added Elder Monson. And Elder Packer summarized, "There was a kind and forgiving nature which somehow seemed counterpoint to his fiery sermons. To him it was one thing to vigorously condemn in general every form of transgression. But in particular with an individual, it was different. There emerged a gentle, forgiving spirit that was truly Christlike."

The Tabernacle Choir's renditions of "The Lord's Prayer," "O My Father," and "I Know That My Redeemer Lives" touched all who listened. But it was Mark's favorite song, based on Alfred Lord Tennyson's "Crossing the Bar," that expressed best his feelings for the time when he truly saw "his Pilot face to face."

Mark had never feared death. He always said that the Lord could take him when He wanted him, and meanwhile he would not worry. The one possibility that had concerned him had been that he would lose his mental capacities. Now he had been blessed to the end, having been able to work in his office less than a week before he died.

As Dorene began to sort through his papers after the funeral, she found in the top drawer of his desk a piece of newsprint covered with his familiar handwriting. There was no explanation with it, no reason given for his having kept it, no source for the poem that he had scribbled. Somewhere, at some time in his life, he had found a poem that touched his heart and expressed his feelings. Part of that poem, in his own handwriting and with his own spelling, reads:

> *I folo a famous father,*
> *His honor is mine to wear.*
> *He gave me a name that was free from shame,*
> *A name he was proud to bear . . .*

> *I folo a famous father,*
> *And never a day goes by*
> *But I feel that he looks down on me*
> *To carry his standard high.*

Now Mark Edward Petersen's family "folos" a famous father.

Index